Glimpses of Stornoway

A light covering of history in words and pictures from Viking times to the 1950s (with the occasional mention of later on!)

Cromwell Street on Market Day c 1914

Lews Castle in 1878

The publication of *Glimpses of Stornoway* is backed by the Stornoway Amenity Trust and The Stornoway Trust. *Glimpses of Stornoway* is based on work which began with the historical series of calendars and booklets developed by the Stornoway Trust, Stornoway Amenity Trust and Intermedia Services since 2002

First published in Great Britain in 2009 by Intermedia Services   ISBN 978-0-9563138-0-5

© Intermedia Services 2009

Compiled, edited and prepared for publication by Fred Silver, Intermedia Services, Stornoway   Printed and bound by Gomer Press, Llandysul, Ceredigion, SA44 4JL

Foreword

This excellent illustrated history of Stornoway adds one more treasure to the ever-growing library of books on our local history.

No apology needs to be given for launching another view of our past on a Hebridean audience avid for each new offering which highlights, both for ourselves and the world-wide Hebridean diaspora, a renewed and justifiable pride in our roots and contribution to the international scene.

The genesis of this highly readable publication lies with the work of the Stornoway Amenity Trust, so generously supported by the Stornoway Trust, and with the annual production of that much acclaimed and widely sought-after publication, the Stornoway Amenity Trust Calendar. The book has also developed from a booklet about the history of Stornoway, funded by the Stornoway Trust and published in 2004, as well as other booklets published by the Amenity Trust on various local topics.

Fred Silver helped to create the calendars and the booklets and has skilfully married some of the pictures from them and from elsewhere with an absorbing and fascinating text, some created from his own research and the remainder from the work of others mentioned in the comprehensive bibliography.

I believe this is the first such publication and have no doubt the book will secure for itself a warm reception wherever it goes and will be doubly acceptable not only on its own merits but also because it has been devised by one of our own adopted sons whose affection for Lewis and its people breathes from each page.

The fact that the educative and charming vignettes in *Glimpses of Stornoway* have been compiled by an incomer to the island is very much a bonus, for despite his affection for his new homeland, Fred Silver has brought that necessary degree of detachment and objectivity so essential for accurate and acceptable local history.

I have had immense pleasure and added information from reading a preview of Fred Silver's book and I commend it to all who enjoy and value good reading and the mind-opening experience of well-chosen illustrations.

Sandy Matheson,

Lord Lieutenant of the Western Isles

`The picture of the Fish Mart on the cover was taken by former Stornoway Provost Sandy Matheson in November 1971.
He used a Pentax SLR camera with a 105mm lens and his vantage point was the Town Hall clock tower.

The compilation and publication of this book has been supported by The Stornoway Trust and the Stornoway Amenity Trust

The Stornoway Trust: In 1923 Lord Leverhulme – at the time when he put the island of Lewis up for sale – gifted Lews Castle and 64,000 acres of land to the people of Stornoway parish and the Stornoway Trust was established to manage this substantial estate on behalf of the community. The Trust is a community landowner, democratically elected by the entire electorate living on the estate and remains – by a great margin – the largest community landowner in terms of population in Scotland.

Stornoway Amenity Trust: The Trust was set up in 1994 with the aim of providing improvements in the town of Stornoway. It has been involved in creating floral displays in the town centre; various environmental improvements and improved signage; the provision of festive lighting and events; the development of the Stornoway Waterwheel and Visitor Centre; the restoration of the Lady Matheson monument; the holding of a summer street market; and the publication of postcards, souvenirs and booklets.

Index and contents

Royal visits but not as we know them ....early kings in Lewis and conflicts with the Scots and Norse 5-9

Industry starts to develop but there's another battle ....first maps and the Cromwellian onslaught 9-11

Coin hoards hidden in the Castle Grounds ....different millennia, different conflicts, but same idea – bury the cash 12-13

School brings "civilitie" to town ....17th and 18th centuries see developments in learning and work 21-20

Pictures and images across the centuries ....various views of the town and its activities including the original meal mill 21-28

Local money – Stornoway's own notes ....why the last Mackenzie landowner printed his own money 28-29

A Miscellany of Stornoway I ....pictures and snippets from across the centuries 30-33

Maps of central Stornoway ....two views of the streets and quays in 1821 and 1851 34-35

Catching whales in Stornoway harbour ....tradition of community whale hunts lasts through the 19th century 36-37

South Beach to North Beach – the old town ....house by house search for history and people from the past 38-46

The great years of the herring fishery ....town was part of the world's greatest fishery as port grew 47-51

Views of Stornoway in 19th and early 20th centuries ....pictures of the town, and the Lews Castle Grounds 52-56

Stornoway takes to the High Seas ....the role of the town and its people in the great clipper races 57-59

Lews Castle and The Nicolson Institute in pictures ....inside the Castle as it once was and the school as it began 60-61

The Matheson era in Stornoway Industry ....the town as a centre for varied industrial development 62-63

Peat experiments prove bad for fish ....scientists put town at forefront of oil-from-peat technology 64-66

Memories of Donald Munro ....the ill-famed factor, the flower show and the insurance company 67-68

Campaign for new mill fails after blaze ....crofters protest for years after Willowglen mill burns down 69-70

Challenges and developments for the town's harbour ....how harbour authorities copied with soaring demand 71-73

Rise and fall of the Poorhouse ....the building of the Poorhouse and how it worked 74-75

Burning out the town's heart ....the rise, fall and rise of Stornoway's Town Hall 77-79

The town in peace and war in pictures ....various views of the town and its surrounds 80-82

The cinema comes to Stornoway ....the role of the flicks in social life after 1899 83-84

Stornoway slang ....a collection of local words made by the late Norman M Macdonald 85-86

The Metagama and other views ....photographs looking back at 1902-1953 87-90

A Miscellany of Stornoway II ....snippets from across the centuries 91

A town for tweed ....the rise and fall of the Harris Tweed industry in Stornoway 93-94

Cromwell Street, past and present ....a glance at the shops of the Narrows over the years 95

Views over the town from the air ....Stornoway's changes as seen from above 95-97

The Lewis Pipe Band ....music in the streets with the pipers down the years 98

A Miscellany of Stornoway III ....pictures and snippets from across the centuries 99-101

Cuddy Point, Matheson Memorial, ...plans, developments and restoration 102-103

Acknowledgments and bibliography ....a big thank you to all those whose work and assistance helped create this book 104

Royal visits ... but not as we know them!

In modern times it is the names of Hebridean islands like Harris, Barra or Eriskay that have become widely known but in the Norse era of island history, Lewis was pre-eminent. It is, for instance, the only Hebridean island mentioned individually in the Orkneyinga Saga, with the rest being referred to as the Sudreyjar or Southern Isles.

While Stornoway itself is not named in documents until the 15th Century, it must clearly have been central to island life at that time as it had been thousands of years earlier for the builders of the huge stone structures on Gallow's Hill and elsewhere around Broad Bay.

Quite when the Norse kingdom of the Isles emerged is not exactly known, but almost all the placenames on Lewis – like Stornoway – have a Nordic origin and away from the coasts many involve the element "bolstadr" or "stadr": indicating homestead or farm, implying a great depth of early settlement in Lewis.

A key record of Irish history, now known as the Annals of the Four Masters, records that in 853, "Gothfrith, son of Fergus, chieftain of the Hebrides, died".

In 989, the Annals of Ulster report that "Gudrod, king of the Hebrides," had been slain, while the battle of Clontarf in 1014 involved warriors "from Man, from Lewis, from Skye" as well as Orkney, Kintyre and Argyll, according to Njal's Saga.

The kingdom of Man and the Isles was created by chieftains and armies from the Hebrides led by Harald the Black of Islay and his son, Godred Crovan. Godred finally won control of the Isle of Man in 1079 at the battle of Skyhill using an army raised in the Hebrides.

One of the earliest detailed references to Lewis comes in the Chronicles of the Kings of Man and the Isles, which give some detail of the struggle between the local rulers and the Norwegian kings.

Written in Latin, and known from manuscripts dating from the 14th Century, this monastic chronicle records how in 1097, King Magnus of Norway sent Ingemund to be king of the Isles. "Cumque ad insulam Leodus pervenisset" writes the chronicler "On reaching the Isle of Lewis"

Ingemund "sent envoys to all the chieftains of the Isles, instructing them to hold a convention and make him king. But in the meantime he himself and his associates indulged in rapine and orgies, violating the chastity of matrons and maidens and gave themselves up to every other variety of entertainment and pleasure of the flesh. When the chieftains, who were already assembled together to set him on the throne, heard about this, they were greatly incensed. They came upon him by night and setting fire to his house, they either burned or put to the sword both him and his companions."

Angered by this reaction to his appointee, King Magnus and his army came in force across the North Sea the following year and laid waste not only to Lewis but the rest of the Outer Hebrides. Interestingly, Magnus became known as "Barelegs" or "Berrføtt" in later years because he admired the shorter style of man's dress worn by Hebrideans which showed the lower legs, and then used it himself. However, in 1098 he was eager to remind the local population who was in charge. The Heimskringla – or Chronicles of the Kings of Norway – tells how he attacked Lewis and then the other isles "killing the people and plundering wherever he came with his men."

The country people fled in all directions, the chronicle says, some "into Skotlandsfjörd" the Norse name for the Minch; some to Kintyre and Ireland, while others simply joined with Magnus' army. The onslaught was celebrated in verse – in modern translation, the poem begins:

"In Lewis Isle with fearful blaze

The house-destroying fire plays;

To hills and rocks the people fly

Fearing all shelter but the sky"

And concludes:

"And many an island-girl's wail

Was heard as through the isle we strife sail."

It is perhaps relevant that modern genetic research shows that, while the men of the Faroes and Iceland came from Norway, the women originated from the Hebrides.

It was a mistranslation of the verse above which reinforced the myth of the Vikings burning the forests of Lewis. What they clearly did in reality was to destroy the precious roof timbers of many homes. Pieces of wood big enough for roof timbers were scarce all across the Norse region and much prized. The Icelandic sagas tell how settlements in that island were established by colonists from Norway who took some of their prized house timbers with them, and let them drift ashore as a way of establishing a fortunate location for their new dwellings.

Only a few years previously, in England, another leader with Nordic origins, King William I, swept with full force through northern England. The "Harrying of the North" was to suppress the first major rebellion after his invasion from Normandy in 1066. The attack was so destructive that the Domesday Book of landholdings, compiled in 1086, described many parts of the formerly prosperous region simply as being wasteland. If the impact on Magnus' army on Lewis was similar, this loss of resources might form the background to the problems of the next known kingly involvement with Lewis.

In 1187, the Isle of Man Chronicle tells how Godred, King of the Isles, died, leaving three sons, transcribed by the chronicler as Reginald, Olaf and Ivar. Reginald took over as King of the Isles in 1188 although his father had preferred Olaf. Reginald awarded the island of Lewis to Olaf. The chronicler agrees that Lewis is the biggest of all the islands but describes it as sparsely populated "and because of its mountainous and rocky character it does not lend itself to cultivation. The inhabitants…live by hunting and fishing." Olaf, who was only ten when his father died, moved to Lewis and is described as ending up "living the life of a pauper." He became alarmed by his "poor sustenance" and "how little his army was being fed" and so in 1207 he went to his brother to plead for a better portion of the kingdom. His brother listened to the plea and told Olaf he would get an answer the next day; but when he was summoned before the King the following morning, he was arrested and sent to jail in Scotland under the control of King William 1. He stayed in jail for seven years until he was freed after the death of King William. He then went on a pilgrimage to a shrine in Spain with a "none too insignificant retinue" of nobles and returned to be greeted "affectionately" by his brother. King Reginald now persuaded him to marry Lauon, from Kintyre, sister of Reginald's wife, and he returned to Lewis with her. Soon after that, the chronicle says that Olaf was visited by Reginald, Bishop of the Isles, another close relative, and Bishop Reginald promptly annulled the marriage on the grounds that Olaf had had a relationship with Lauon's first cousin. Since Olaf went on to marry Christina, daughter of the Earl of Ross, establishing a direct mainland alliance, this sounds as if it was a direct and deliberate act of defiance by Olaf.

Certainly, it annoyed King Reginald's wife who promptly ordered her son Godred, chieftain in the Isle of Skye, to murder Olaf. However, the local sheriff, Paul Balkisson objected, joined Olaf and ultimately they ambushed Godred and his men on St Columba's Isle in Loch Snizort, Skye, where the cathedral of the Bishop of the Isles stood (it was in use from 1079 to 1498). They crossed the loch at night and attacked about at nine in the morning, and "cut down all whom they found outside the confines of the church." Godred was captured and cruelly mutilated. This began a civil war across the islands between the brothers which lasted until Reginald was killed in battle in 1228. Olaf then reigned for nine years.

For Lewis, the final episode of kingly attention from outside of what is now Scotland came in 1263 when King Haakon of Norway reasserted Norway's control of Lewis and the rest of the Hebrides. This followed yet another lengthy period of disorder in the Kingdom of the Isles, provoked partly by the Macdougalls, descendants of the great Hebridean warrior and leader Somerled, operating from Dunollie Castle, near Oban, first built by Somerled himself. With the scale of his fleet and his army, Haakon attempted to emulate the assault by Magnus Barelegs which had taken him as far as North Wales – and his impact was such that Kyleakin – Kyles Haakon – remains in Skye as a memory of his visit.

Earlier in the 1200s, King Alexander II of Scotland began to try to expand Scottish influence over the Isles. The Norwegian account of Haakon's expedition tells how John MacDougall, King of the Isles, was called to meet Alexander II and asked to switch his allegiance from Norway to Scotland. John refused and retreated back into his domain. The Norwegian account says: "All King John's relations and friends pressed him to assent. But he behaved well, and uprightly; and declared that he would not break his oath to King Haakon. On this King John went away, and stopped not at any place till he came quite north to Lewis." Clearly Lewis was seen as a good place to avoid the immediate impact of any counter-blast from King Alexander and it is reasonable to assume that an early version of Stornoway castle out in the bay would have been King John's refuge. King Alexander II died during his subsequent campaign to try to take over the Hebrides and his young son, Alexander III, took over the kingship. There was therefore a gap before the efforts to gain control of the Hebrides resumed. Around 1260 various diplomatic approaches were made to Haakon but he rebuffed all offers and launched his expedition.

Skye, in particular, was under attack from the mainland, Haakon had been told. The Norwegian account states "In summer there came letters from the Kings of the Hebrides in the western seas. They complain'd much of the hostilities which the Earl of Ross, Kiarnach, the son of Mac-camal, and other Scots committed in the Hebrides when they went out to Skye. They burned villages, and churches, and they killed great numbers both of men and women.

"They affirmed, that the Scotch had even taken the small children and raising them on the points of their spears, shook them till they fell down to their hands, when they threw them away lifeless on the ground. They said also, that the Scottish King purposed to subdue all the Hebrides, if life was granted him."

Haakon's expedition descended upon Orkney and Caithness and then he "sailed with all his forces to a haven that is called Asleifarvic, from that to Lewis, so on to Raasay, and, from thence to that place, in Skye-sound, which is called Callach-stane" – possibly Caisteal Moil off Kyleakin. He was there joined by forces from the Isle of Man and elsewhere. Later he heard that John, King of the Hebrides, had changed sides; there was a conflict at Largs with the forces of King Alexander and Haakon returned to Orkney where he took ill and died. This was also the death of the Norse supremacy. Three years later Lewis and the rest of the Hebrides were transferred to Scotland by the Treaty of Perth. The next monarch to visit Stornoway would be Scottish.

Another Royal visit and battle for future of Stornoway

The Hebridean connections with the Isle of Man and with Norway that were established in the Viking era endured for centuries after the area became part of the Scottish kings' realm in 1266 – and formed a cultural basis for the continuing concept of the Lordship of the Isles.

For instance, as late as 1368, the King of Norway was reminding the King in Edinburgh that part of the Hebridean handover deal involved an annual payment of 100 marks to Norway; the churches of the Isles remained the responsibility of the Archbishop of Trondheim in Norway until 1472, and when Dean Donald Munro wrote his "A Description Of The Western Isles Of Scotland", published in 1549, the first island in his list was the Isle of Man.

It could be said that this vision of difference culminated in the way that John, the last Lord of the Isles, negotiated the Treaty of Westminster-Ardtornish (1462) with Edward IV of England, proposing to divide Scotland between himself, the Earl of Douglas and Edward IV. It was the revelation of this deal that led to the Lordship's lands, which then included Stornoway and Lewis, being confiscated by the King of Scots, James IV, in 1493.

Throughout the years that followed, James and his successor attempted to tie the local leaders into leases and agreements for their lands, culminating in the visit to

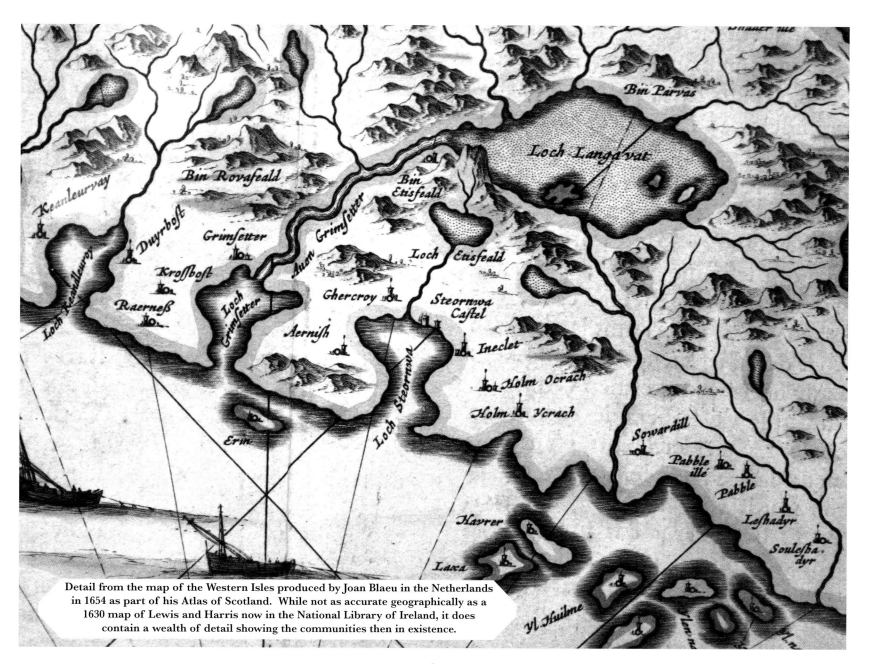

Detail from the map of the Western Isles produced by Joan Blaeu in the Netherlands in 1654 as part of his Atlas of Scotland. While not as accurate geographically as a 1630 map of Lewis and Harris now in the National Library of Ireland, it does contain a wealth of detail showing the communities then in existence.

Stornoway of King James V in 1540. This was clearly intended to make a point. It involved a fleet of 12 ships, and included the Earls of Huntley and Arran with 1000 of their men, and the King's trusted advisor, Cardinal David Beaton, Archbishop of St Andrews and the last Scottish Cardinal before the Scottish Reformation. He was backed by a force of 500 men. In addition, there were the King's own man plus "many barons and gentlemen" with their servants. King James was clearly prepared for a very warm welcome indeed! However, there was no resistance but, as a precaution, the King took local leader Ruari Macleod back to Edinburgh with him.

Stornoway was now firmly on the Scottish map. The first surviving detailed account written about the area came from Sir Donald Monro, High Dean of the Isles, who wrote a brief account of all the islands, which appeared in 1549.

Describing the island of Lewis and Harris, he wrote "Lewis is the north pairt of this ile, and the maist also, faire and weill inhabit at the coste, ane fertile fruitfull countrey, for the most part all beire [bere, an early variety of barley] , with 4 paroche kirks, and with ane castell callit Steornaway."

He goes on to explain that herring were plentiful in the sea lochs, including Loch Stornoway. There were eight salmon rivers and on the moors and in the glens there were many sheep which always lived outside and were shorn once a year in the sheepfolds. Whales were often caught, he reports, and there was a particular cove where people would gather to catch a range of fish including whiting and haddock.

This is the first indication of outside interest in local resources – and over the following years, as troubles continued with the Macleod chiefs, Stornoway became a greater focus of royal concern, culminating in the battles with the Fife Adventurers.

In 1597 an Act was passed by the Scottish Parliament, the preamble of which alleged that the Lords of the district neglected to develop the rich fisheries in their possession as well as failing to perform the services due by them to the Crown. A further Act allowed for the setting up of three new Royal Burghs, including one at Stornoway. King James VI had tired of his tumultuous and warring chiefs in Lewis and now wanted a complete takeover of their lands. Privy Council records contain a contract between King James VI and a syndicate now remembered as the 'Fife Adventurers'.

These were Patrick of Lindores, James Leirmont of Balcomie, Sir James Anstruther, James Spense of Wormiston, Sir James Sandilands of Seamannamure, Captain William Murray, John Forret of Fincask, Sir William Stewart, Sir George Home and his son David, and Lewis, Duke of Lennox, cousin and favourite of the King. The contract bound the undertakers "to plant policy and civilisation in the hitherto most barren Isle of Lewis, and to develop the extraordinary rich resources of the same for the public good and the Kings profit". Rona, off Lewis, the Shiant Isles, and Trotternish in north Skye were also part of the deal with the Adventurers.

Confiscation of island lands was the clear aim – the document stipulated that "no part of the Highlands or Isles should thereafter, at any time, be disponit in few, tack or uterways but to Lowland men" or at least to such Highlanders as could find Lowland "cautioners".

Towards the end of 1598 the Fife Adventurers set out for Lewis, led by the Duke of Lennox, and backed by five or six hundred picked mercenaries and well armed Lowlanders. The Lowlanders created an encampment in Stornoway. They built houses of stone, timber and turf, about where South Beach Street is today, on the foreshore. The Macleod castle offshore (its site is underneath No 1 pier) was besieged and fell to the invaders by December.

However, the Macleod leaders Murdoch and Neil began a fightback. Murdoch Macleod took to the seas. Neil remained in Lewis to make guerrilla warfare against the colonists, who found themselves short of provisions because the natives had cleared the Island of supplies. Their shelter was also inadequate and the winter weather was setting in. The colonists decided to send one of their members, James Leirmont of Balcomie, to inform the King of their progress and to obtain a supply of provisions.

On 7th December 1598 Murdoch Macleod with a small fleet of a galley and two birlinns attacked Balcomie's ship off the coast of Ross-shire, killing or making prisoner all of those on board. When news reached Lewis that the Laird of Balcomie had been captured, the colonists sent Colonel Stewart Spence of Wormiston and others to carry out the mission to Edinburgh.

Taking advantage of the reduction in the numbers of defenders, Neil Macleod suddenly attacked the colonists with what was said to be 200 barbarous 'bluidie and wiket

Heilandmen' armed with bows and arrows, two handed swords, pistols and other weapons. They killed 22 of the colonists, burnt property valued at 20,000 marks and carried off horses, cows, oxen, sheep and other things worth £10,000.

The plan for the colony had envisaged the building of four churches and the setting up on a local court or Stewartry, independent of Inverness. And, in an attempt to prevent the sea-borne disaster which befell the colonists, the Islanders had been instructed to destroy all their galleys and birlinns, something which clearly could not be enforced.

The colonists, however, struck back by doing a deal with Neil by which he betrayed his brother who was captured and later tried and executed. The scheme for a settlement in Lewis was extended to include 10 churches and as many burgh townships as they pleased to set up.

The colonists proceeded to plan their town – along the Point of Stornoway – and devised what was described by Sir Robert Gordon as a "prettie town" although they were also careful to fortify it. A charter of 1607 describes the "villam de Stroneway" as lying on the shore adjoining the old castle. However, long before that was drawn up, the weakness of the colony had been exposed. In 1601, Neil Macleod turned against the colonists and killed 50 or 60 of them after an ambush.

On the mainland, Mackenzie of Kintail, who had long wanted to expand his possessions to include Lewis, released Tormod Macleod, son of the previous chief, and he returned to Lewis to rally resistance. Tormod and Neil then led a force which devastated the new town again, and killed or captured all the colonists. Two of the leaders were held as hostages on Lewis and the rest sent back to Edinburgh – the hostages were surety for an agreement that all their claims on Lewis were cancelled.

King James VI tried desperately to persuade the Convention of Estates of Scotland to fund a new attack on Lewis. (This was a sister institution to the Scottish Parliament which sat from the early sixteenth century. Initially it was only attended by the clergy and nobles, but burgh commissioners were later added.) The Convention turned him down.

He then attempted to raise an army throughout the Highlands for an invasion – which met with little enthusiasm – and finally returned to the Adventurers to agree they would raise forces for a further effort. However, in 1603 James VI became King James I of England as well – and this distracted him from Lewis for a couple of years.

However, by 1605 James VI was back on the case – and now not only the "havers, keepers and deteiners of castell, tour and fortalice of Sternoway" but the owners of other castles in the islands were his targets. He was not going to be made a fool of by "sic a unfamous byke of lawless lymmaris" (such a wasps' nest of lawless vagabonds).

A second expedition of Adventurers, although most of the original group had dropped out, sailed to Lewis in August 1605. They were also supported by mainland nobles like Mackenzie of Kintail, with his own aims in mind. They did a deal with Tormod Macleod, who was sent to London and ended up in prison, and they then took over the island again. The new colony was left with a good force of soldiers to defend it who successfully defied attacks over the winter from Neil Macleod. Spring 1606 started well for the colonists, provisions arrived, building went on, and land was prepared for sowing.

Then money started to run short, skilled workers left and soldiers started to desert. By summer, the colonists were pleading for help from the mainland to counter the attacks from the local people. In September Mackenzie of Kintail was asked to descend with "fire and sword" on the Hebrides after forces from Clanranald in Uist and MacNeil in Barra assailed the colony and "committit barbarous and detestable murthouris and slaughteris upon thame."

April 1607 saw another assault on the colony from Neil Macleod. By this time, a number of villages had been constructed around Stornoway, Neil Macleod now sought out the colony leaders and announced he had changed his mind. The scheme would be good for the island and he would like to join in, he told them. The colonists were won over and Neil even assumed control of their security. For many of the Lowlanders, this was their last mistake. By night, 300 heavily armed Lewismen entered the camp and slaughtered the colonists as they slept. In all, £10,000 of damage was done as the main houses of the settlement were burned out.

James VI was not amused. He promptly ordered the Duke of Huntly to pacify the islands in a year "not by agreement with the countrey people, bot by extirpatioun of thame." With this proposal for a scorched earth policy, it seems the King was aiming to pick up where Norway's King Magnus "Barelegs" had left off in 1098.

However, this plan became bogged down in national politics as Huntly was under fire for remaining a Roman Catholic. Meanwhile more Island chiefs were joining in. Ruari Macleod of Harris arrived with a strong force and took over Stornoway Castle and other fortifications. The Privy Council ordered him to leave on pain of death, so he did only for Neil Macleod to return on another attack, destroying more of the colony. After what Royal archives describe as incidents of "barbarous cruelty", the surviving colonists fled for a second time.

King James VI (who was at the same time inflicting the same process of colonization on Ulster with effects that remain to this day) gathered himself for a more subtle assault on the Hebrides. Some of the clan leaders were kidnapped, others brought to heel but Neil Macleod remained thrawn and obdurate. A new settlement by colonists began in the winter of 1609 – but Neil and his forces attacked again, killing most and capturing the rest. That was the end of the battle. Colonisation was abandoned.

Mackenzie of Kintail is believed to have covertly assisted Neil in his final campaign against the colony – but for his own ends. Now he was able to buy out the remaining Adventurers and was authorized by the King to pacify Lewis. He arrived with overwhelming force – perhaps 700 men – and met little resistance. Neil Macleod remained at large in west Lewis – until in 1612 he took refuge with Ruari Macleod of Harris, who gave him up to the King. Neil was executed in Edinburgh in 1613. Over 12 years, Stornoway had been the setting for what amounted to a civil war. Now the shattered town was to get a chance to expand in peace for a few years.

Industry starts to develop but there's one more battle

The history of Stornoway as it developed over recent centuries can be seen in outline within a few years of the Mackenzie era beginning after 1613. Colin, Lord Kintail and, from 1623, Earl of Seaforth was anxious to develop the islands in the way that the Adventurers had seen as possible. The search was on for natural resources and outside investment. Records suggest, for instance, that there were copper and lead mines in Lewis in the 17th century and iron ore was being extracted in the 18th century. Fisheries were the main concern, however, but before work on all this could get going, Stornoway was to see another major battle fought in its streets.

Far more is known about Lewis and Stornoway from studies done by outsiders at the time. For instance, the notes accompanying the 1654 map of the islands created by Joseph Blaeu, the Dutch mapmaker, tell how: "On that coast of the island of Lewis which faces south east, two gulfs of the sea break into the land, of which one is called the South Loch, the other the North Loch. Each supplies an abundance of fish for catching all year." The notes were based on surveys done in the first years of the 17th Century and state that Lewis has: "four churches, one castle, seven largish rivers and twelve smaller ones in addition, all according to their size producing salmon: in very many places the sea penetrates the land and spreads into gulfs, all abundantly supplying herring. There is here great production of sheep, which wander freely on moors." The map clearly shows Stornoway and nearby Inacleit along with many other familiar village names across Lewis. Another, far more geographically accurate map dated 1630 and preserved in the National Library of Ireland, clearly identifies Stornoway as a major point of reference and the site of a church along with the Ui church at Aignish.

In 1630, as part of a long legal battle by Lord Seaforth to get trading privileges for Stornoway, a survey of Lewis and Stornoway was undertaken by Captain John Dymes for the Privy Council. At that point King Charles I was supporting Seaforth's bid for full burgh status against opposition from other towns like Inverness who feared additional competition. Captain Dymes says: "The climate is something colder than ours here in England but the ayre very wholesome as doth appear by the healthfull bodyes and long lives of the inhabitants." He says there were people of 100 and even 120 years of age and even one that he claims local people "did affirme unto me" was 180 years old – this sounds rather as if the great island tradition of telling tall tales to outsiders was already well-established!

He is on sounder ground with what he could actually see around him – plentiful fish, especially herring, cod and ling, as well as whales. Barley and oats were being grown on arable land around the coasts and lochs. He says Lewis had about 20 townships of around ten cottages and a total of 4,000 people, many of whom had been settled in the island by Lord Seaforth since he took over.

The commodities produced on the island were basically cattle and "some Pladinge or Tartan which is a kind of woollen cloath wherewith they cloath themselves." However, "the great and rich commodity" available, but which the islanders were failing to exploit, was fishing. There were "not above a dozen boates" which "doe kill anie fish for sale." Dutch herring fishermen with their well-organised herring busses had been working off the islands since 1628 and had made as much as £7500 in three months selling their catch in Europe. The Dutch were resident in Stornoway with a factor and workforce of six based in the town. They had a storehouse and a "pretty dwelling house." The islanders were more accustomed to subsistence or chance harvests from the seas – for instance, around 100 whales had been captured and killed in the lochs in 1629 and the meat preserved by smoking, as they did not have salt available.

Captain Dymes praises the excellence of Stornoway harbour for shipping in all weathers, and also the way it is easily defended. He points out that Stornoway's open location means that it gets the sun all day; both "fire and water" are easily available, presumably from the peat cutting which he also describes and from local wells, and he adds it was "alsoe the place which hath bene always most frequented both of the inhabitants and strangers."

In the town itself, he says there are "already some fewe buildings" and Lord Seaforth was building a church.

Quite what Stornoway looked like during or after the battles 20 years earlier is not known but a plan of the town does exist from the period of the Cromwellian occupation in the 1650s. It would not be unreasonable to assume that the grid street pattern still shown by Point Street and its offshoots like Bank Street and Castle Street reflect the original planned settlement and that Cromwell's soldiers, rather than starting from scratch, strengthened and extended the earlier defences. The plan, which shows the defences in detail but the rest of the town only in sketch form, shows St Lennan's church, a large house which it describes as the Manor House, a variety of warehouses, and what is termed a "brewing house".

The army of the Commonwealth, which had tried and executed King Charles only four years before, descended on Stornoway in 1653 to crush a would-be rebellion in support of the Stuart monarchy by the 3rd Earl of Seaforth, Kenneth Mòr, then a rash, hot-headed 18-year-old. Cromwell also wished to forestall a Royalist plan to cede Lewis to the Netherlands in return for more support. At that time the Commonwealth was at war with the Dutch.

According to John Knox, of the British Fisheries Society, writing in 1786, several Dutch families settled in Stornoway in the previous century "on account of the fisheries, but they were unfortunately driven away, during the war between England and Holland" which would have left accommodation vacant in the town.

The Roundhead expeditionary force, involving six troop companies backed by warships and supply vessels landed on August 16, 1653. Commanded by Colonel Ralph Cobbett, these men were part of the most professional army ever raised in Britain and were among the forces commanded by General George Monck, one of Britain's most successful commanders on land and sea of any era. Lewis was

subdued after some brief skirmishes and Colonel Cobbett left with some of the forces, leaving Major Peter Crispe in charge of four troop companies backed up by several warships.

Fortifications were erected or strengthened – ditches 20 feet wide and 15 feet deep provided defensive cover, one running from where the Town House (Golden Ocean) is today across what is now Cromwell Street under where Macneils pub stands. There was some sort of gate structure across Point Street and then the moat cut straight to the shore on South Beach. A similar moat ran across the peninsula to the west, kinking round the west end of St Lennan's church and running into South Beach underneath where the Star Inn now is. Unless these ditches already existed from earlier battles, the material dug out of them must have gone somewhere and may have formed part of the defences elsewhere.

These defences soon faced a formidable test from the forces of the Mackenzies backed by Colonel Norman Macleod of Raasay, a relative of Lord Seaforth. Around 400 to 500 men, organised in two columns attacked the Cromwellian soldiers, some of whom were quartered in the town outside the main defences, as there was only room for 200 men in the church. Colonel Macleod had landed at Loch Shell several days earlier and had managed to arrive on the outskirts of Stornoway unseen, perhaps aided by local guides and winter darkness. The attacker also had inside knowledge, reputedly supplied by John Morison, the tacksman of Bragar. He published a study and memoir of the islands in 1680. He says Seaforth's forces killed many of Cromwell's men "but being destitute of artillery, could not storm the garrison, notwithstanding that he assaulted the trenches, neither would they be drawn out to the fields to encounter." The area between the gateway across Point Street and what is now Francis Street and running across much of the peninsula was then low-lying marsh which could be flooded to provide additional defence.

According to the Traditions of the Morrisons (collected by Captain F W L Thomas in the 19th Century) John Morrison was on friendly terms with the Cromwellian officers and spent the evening before the midnight attack drinking and playing cards with them. He then reported back to his brother Alan who was organising part of the attacking force, and gave details of where the sentries were posted and how the defences were organised.

Seen right is the only surviving plan of the Cromwellian fortifications for Stornoway, which may have been based on the ones used only 40 years before by the Fife Adventurers. The outline plan dates from late 1653 and is preserved in the library of Worcester College, Oxford. It shows the layout before the construction of the Cromwellian citadel further down the point in 1654. A hand written key to the symbols is given on the original map. A summary of the descrptions has been added to the map.

The handwriting in the centre reads: "The groundplan of the fortifications at Stornoway upon Lewis Island.

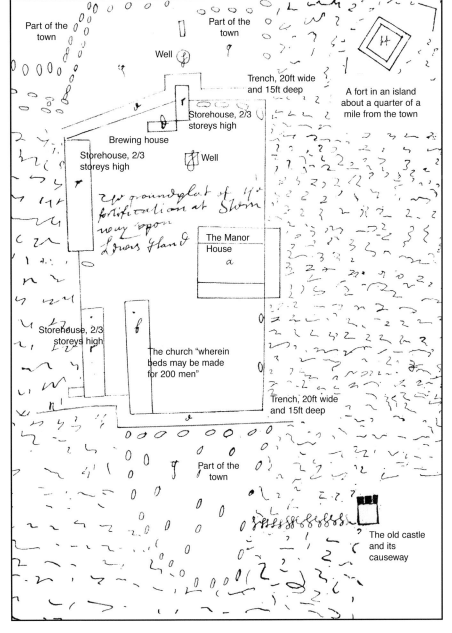

Part of the town

Part of the town

Well

Trench, 20ft wide and 15ft deep

A fort in an island about a quarter of a mile from the town

Storehouse, 2/3 storeys high

Brewing house

Storehouse, 2/3 storeys high

Well

The groundplat of ye fortification at Stornoway upon Lewis Island

The Manor House

Storehouse, 2/3 storeys high

The church "wherein beds may be made for 200 men"

Trench, 20ft wide and 15ft deep

Part of the town

The old castle and its causeway

After the failure of the attack, the Cromwellian soldiers joined the remnants of the Macleod supporters to impose swift reprisals on the population. Not much is known about this, but if reports of a contemporary attack on Dundee are anything to go by, the terror would have been horrific.

The attack led to the defences being strengthened and a citadel being built at the end of Point Street. Remnants of these structures remain in other places, such as Inverness and Leith, and if it was on the same scale, this could have been a large, square, three storey building. It seems to have absorbed almost all the stonework of the old Castle out in the bay and was built in an area described on the 1653 map as part of the town with quite a number of dwellings sketched on it.

Both the citadel and the destruction of the old Castle were remembered long afterwards. John Morrison said in 1680 that "the old Castle of Stornoway (was) but lately broken down by the English garrison in Cromwell's time." In 1695 Martin Martin, reporting on his visit to Stornoway, said: "The castle at Stornvay village was destroyed by the English garrison, kept there by Oliver Cromwell." A Captain Barlow reported in 1753: "There is the remains of an old fort built by Oliver Cromwell, which was demolished by the English garrison when they were withdrawn from that country in the reign of King Charles II." The First Statistical Account of Lewis in 1796 records that "on a small point near the town there is a vestige remaining of a castle built for the protection of the place by the Macleods, the ancient possessors of the island. Not far from it there was another tower built by Cromwell to awe the neighbourhood. No part of this one remains." In the 1870s Captain F W L Thomas, author of a variety of historical works on island history and traditions, reported that the tower had been located behind what is now Amity House. In 1911, "the remains of rubble-work, about 8ft thick, were found about 2 or 3ft from the surface, in the course of some drain repairs" in that area.

After 1660, with the old castle reduced to the fragment that remained until the building of No 1 pier, and Cromwell's tower doubtless reused for other buildings, the military period of Stornoway's history came to an end. Seaforth Lodge, the new residence of the Mackenzies across the harbour was not a fortress although it was still well-located to maintain a watch for any approaching fleet!

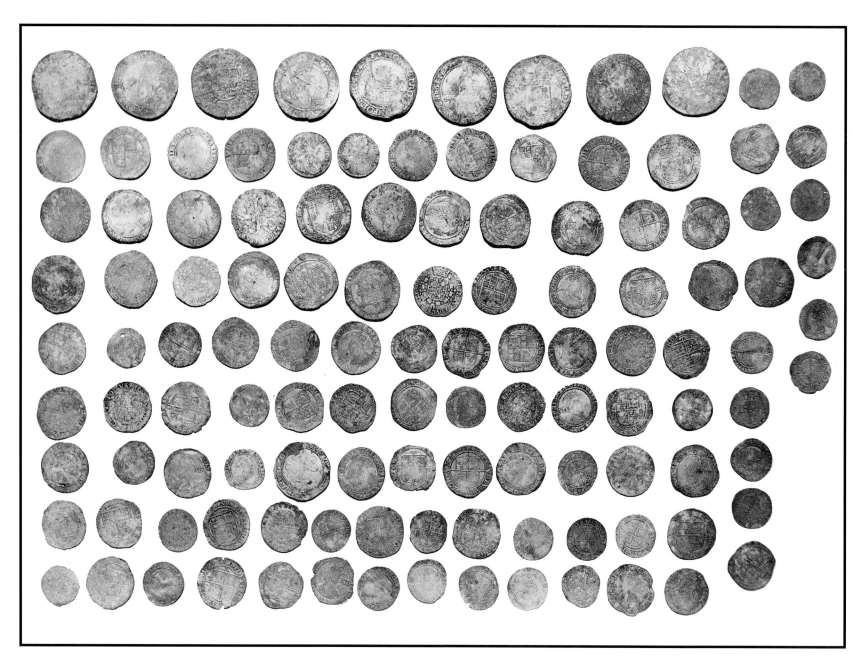

Coin hoards hidden in Castle Grounds

In July 1954, a hoard of coins – pictured on the left – was found in the Castle Grounds, by Shoe Glen (so named because when people used to walk to Stornoway from the country, they would walk barefooted, with their shoes slung around their necks, until they got to the river where they would wash their feet and put on their shoes in order to cross the inner harbour on the huge stepping stones that used to lie there).

The coins were found by a fifteen year-old student of Lews Castle College, John Angus Graham, shortly after the college was opened. All 119 coins, dating from the 16th and 17th century, were found in a small (not more than 11.5 cm in diameter), round clay craggan with moss covering the mouth.

The coins were found to be from England (during the reigns of Elizabeth I, James I and Charles I) and Scotland (during the reigns of James VI and Charles II), but also Ireland, Spain, the Netherlands and Sweden. The latest of the coins, three Charles II merks and one dollar of West Friesland, are all dated 1669, and it is thought that the coins were buried not long after this date. Eleven of these coins are held in the National Museum.

About 40 years later a further hoard dating from around 700 years earlier was found in the same area of the Castle Grounds – this contained 37 items made up mostly of what is called hack-silver cut from ring money.

This find reflects the business of an era when the idea of coinage as such was unfamiliar. Coins were valued only for their weight in silver or gold, and circulated alongside many other forms of precious metal in what is now described as a bullion economy, in which the weight and the purity of the precious metal are what is important, not what form the metal takes.

Far and away the most common metal in the economy was silver, although gold was also used. Silver circulated in the form of bars, or ingots, as well as in the form of jewellery and ornaments. Large pieces of jewellery were often chopped up into smaller pieces known as hack-silver to make up the exact weight of silver required. Imported coins and fragments of coins were also used for the same purpose. Traders carried small scales that could measure weight very accurately, so it was possible to have a very precise system of trade and exchange even without a regular coinage.

The fragments of silver found in the Grounds had all been wrapped in linen and then deposited in a cattle horn. Included in the collection were two Norman coins which date the hoard to around 940-1040 and also point to the trading connections of the Viking era. Normandy, which conquered England in 1066, was founded by Norsemen like the Kingdom of Man and the Isles.

Given the date assigned to the hoard, it might be connected with the report in the Annals of Ulster that in 989 "Gudrod, king of the Hebrides," was slain or victim of the Irish battle of Clontarf in 1014 which involved warriors "from Man, from Lewis, from Skye" as well as Orkney, Kintyre and Argyll, according to Njal's Saga.

School founded in town brings 'civilitie, understanding and knowledge'

In 1680, John Morison, tacksman of Bragar, wrote a description of Lewis in his day. Bere (barley) and oats were widely grown and there was a "multitude of cattle". There were also sheep, goats and horses and a "plentifull forrest" of deer between Loch Seaforth and Harris. Fishing – with herring, cod, ling and salmon along with "all other sorts of smaller fishes" – was the main trade.

Morison also placed great emphasis on the influence of the school established in Stornoway by the Earl of Seaforth. Morison remarks that when he was young, "there was not three in all the countrie that knew" A from B but now most families had at least one who could read and write. "The people fomerlie inclined to rudeness and barbarity, are reduced to cilivilitie, much understanding and knowledge by the flourishing school planted and maintained" by the Seaforths in Stornoway.

In his 1695 book, A Description of the Western Islands of Scotland, Martin Martin, from Skye, wrote: "There is a village called Stornvay, at the head of the bay of that name; it consists of about sixty families; there are some houses of entertainment in it, as also a church and a school, in which Latin and English are taught. The steward of the Lewis hath his residence in this village." The church is presumably St Lennan's, constructed around 1630 and later used as a billet by Cromwell's soldiers. The church appears to have lain across what is now Bank Street, running under the present Royal Bank of Scotland branch and with a graveyard underneath the present Crown Hotel, where remains were found in the 1950s.

Earlier writers commented on the lack of woodlands in Lewis, although several noted the way huge trunks of trees could be found buried in the peat. Martin noted that there were now 100 young birch and hazel trees growing on the south-west of Loch Stornoway – presumably where the Castle Grounds are today. He does not mention a house but it is thought that Lord Seaforth had already established his estate house, Seaforth Lodge, on the Gearraidh Chruaidh, an area of rough sheiling ground on the west side of Stornoway harbour. Parts of this original building can still be seen within the rear of the present Lews Castle. Certainly it was in use by 1719 when some of those involved in that year's Jacobite uprising met there.

By the middle of the 1700s, Stornoway seems to have been a thriving community with a developing civic spirit. For instance, the Freemason's Lodge Fortrose, No. 108, was officially formed on 16 August 1769, having been operating since November 1767. One of their early meeting places was 'on the second feu south of Church Street or Lane on the east side of Oliver Street' (later named Dempster Street and, later still, Cromwell Street). Later, the Brethren were to occupy the present building on Kenneth Street, the foundation stone of which was laid on May 28 1819.

An appeal or "memorial" went in to the Government for the establishment of a Customs Office in Stornoway to deal with the increasing levels of trade. This was granted in 1763 although construction of the Customs House was delayed for some years. By 1781 exports to other ports in Britain included soap, salt, foreign spirits, barrels, slates, kelp, whisky, feathers, hides, skins, wool, woollen yarn, linen, tallow, beef and mutton as well as many different kinds of fish. A Customs cutter was based in Stornoway by 1796 – while a postal service to the mainland had been established in 1756. The postal "packet" as it was termed, carried passengers, horses and cattle as well as mail. The first post-master in Stornoway was Murdoch Mackenzie, father of Colin Mackenzie, of Carn House, who went on to be Surveyor General of India

The first postal vessel was replaced in the 1790s by a new one which crossed weekly. The service was subsidised by the

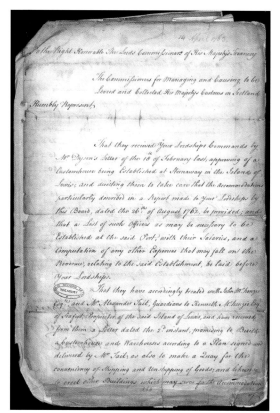
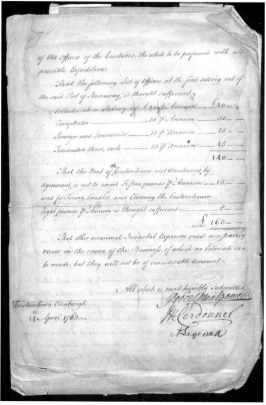

Approval and costings for a Customs post in Stornoway, issued in September 1763. The Customs House at Stornoway was first established in 1707 but was closed in 1737 and transferred to Lochbroom. It was re-established in 1765. Reproduced with permission of the National Archives

Government and the landowner – it cost £130 a year with Seaforth paying £60 and the state £70. (If you compare average earnings in 2008 and 1790, the total subsidy is equivalent to £154,000 in modern money.)

By 1772, the trades of Stornoway – 10 in all – had applied to the Lyon Office and achieved the formal grant of arms for their guilds. The trades involved were ship carpenters, dyers, smiths, shoemakers, tailors, masons, weavers, hecklers (people who combed hemp or flax), coopers (who made barrels) and wrights. At that time, the only other town to have applied for such rights was Aberdeen.

In 1786, John Knox of the British Fisheries Society visited the Hebrides and later wrote a very detailed account of Stornoway as it then was: "The town of Stornoway, rebuilt with houses of stone, lime, and slate, makes a handsome appearance.

"One wing or street is built on a narrow peninsula that stretches out a considerable way into the bay, and adds greatly to the beauty of the landscape. Seaforth Lodge, which is built on a lawn that rises gradually from the head of the bay, and being perfectly white, has a good effect.

"When we came within the harbour, we were sorry to

A detail from an engraving of Stornoway dated 1789 which was prepared for Lord Seaforth. The original was drawn by Lieutenant John Pierce of the Royal Navy. This section shows Seaforth Lodge and the tip of Stornoway. This may reflect the buildings of the time and could suggest that what is now Amity House was already in existence but much of the image is highly stylised.

perceive that noble port without a key [quay]; and it appeared still more strange, when we were informed that £1200 or £1500 had been granted several years ago, by the trustees at Edinburgh, for building a sufficient key, and for raising cottages for fishermen along the shores of the island.

"Something has indeed been erected here in the name of a key, and even that is so much out of repair, that the vessels load and unload upon the beach, or in the bay, by means of boats. In the last century, several Dutch families had settled here on account of the fisheries, but they were unfortunately driven away, during the war between England and Holland.

"Their example had, however, a good effect among the natives, who, from thenceforward, have done more in the way of fishing and traffic than all the West Highlands put together. The late earl of Seaforth, whose good intentions far exceeded his abilities, gave every encouragement in his power for rebuilding and extending the town, and he succeeded as well, that no place between the Mull of Cantire and Cape Wrath contains half its number of inhabitants. It is divided into two towns, one for traders, and the other for fishermen. The first was built close upon the beach, and is accommodated with a church, custom-house, and a good inn.

"Fifty handsome houses have been raised within these last few years, and new ones are still going forward upon a regular plan drawn out by the present proprietor, who favoured me to copy it. The ground is granted on perpetual feus, in lots of fifteen to thirty feet in front, and sixty behind, for a garden , which the inhabitants wish to have increased to double that size, partly on account of the room which their bulky fuel requires. If this could be complied with, the town would increase with great rapidity, and abundantly repay, in the improvement of the island, the concession of fifteen or twenty acres of ground.

"Though the town has suffered greatly by the late wars, its shipping amounts at present to twenty-three decked vessels, which are chiefly employed in the fisheries. That division which is inhabited by fishermen and mechanics, lies at some distance; the street cross each other at right angles, the houses are neat and uniform, accommodated with garden ground, and the whole occupies several acres of good land. Seaforth has it in contemplation to rebuild the church, and erect a gaol and town-house.

"When we arrived at the town, Captain Macleod

expressed a desire to remain that night at an inn, being unwilling, he said, to dress and go for company. This being agreed upon, we sent a card to the factor wishing to see him. In a very short time after, the good woman of the house rushed into the room, calling out, "Seaforth, Seaforth!" and before we could utter a word, Seaforth, who was at her heels, appeared.

"I had the honour of introducing Captain Macleod to him, and we were carried irresistibly to the lodge. When I looked from the window next morning, which happened to be very fine, the views were among the first that I had seen. The small craft were afloat at the head of the bay, with their sails up to dry after some rains; behind, was the point stretching across the bay, and covered to the very extremity with neat white-washed houses. Beyond these, in the outer bay, were the shipping with their sails up; while some were going out, and others coming in.

"Upon the north side of the bay were sloping fields of ripe corn; on the south, were lofty hills; and, to crown this matchless scenery, the far distant mountains of Ross-shire conveyed the idea of a country that had been convulsed into a chaos.

"When the church and the spire shall be built, with a small spire also upon the town-house, and other ornaments which Seaforth's fertile imagination may easily conceive, this place will merit the pencil of the first landscape painter in the kingdom."

During this time Stornoway was a Salt Duty port where ships from many areas of the West Coast had to come for salt which, until 1825, was taxed, sometimes heavily. The salt was stored in the cellar that remains beneath the former Commercial Hotel. The price of salt fell rapidly after the tax was repealed and it became much more easily available, boosting the herring industry.

Stornoway was an active seagoing community, like so many ports. A petition to the Justices of the Peace drafted on Monday 8th November 1790, following a rough night which ended with a riot in Point Street shows how things could get a little out of hand from time to time.

"Upon the Sunday night of the 7th current, a number of sailors belonging to the vessels in the harbour of Stornoway assembled in the public houses in Point Street where they brought a number of women with them. Between seven and eight o'clock they made a most hideous noise and at last

began to fight and blaspheme, by which the whole neighbourhood was disturbed and several of the inhabitants were in danger of their lives, in particular Mur (sic) Macleod, master of the sloop "Venus", who was most inhumanely cut and bruised for attempting to rescue a modest girl they were forcing away with them.

"The riot was entirely owing to the women that associated with them and the Publicans or Innkeepers who sheltered them. Katharine Macleod, alias Cinnamon, is the ringleader of these abandoned women, and in whose room they collect from the different parts of town, and from there they go with some of the men patrolling the streets and to some of the public houses who receive them.

"As most of the men, if not the whole, who were guilty of this riot have now left the place, they cannot be punished," the petitioners admit, but they ask for action against the women involved. They ask the Justices of Peace to fine "Cinnamon" for keeping a "house of bad fame" and otherwise to punish her. They also asked that any others "found guilty of any bad fame" should also be punished "as to your Honours shall seem meet". The innkeepers, it was suggested, should be asked to find sufficient "cautionary" to ensure their good behaviour, and any of them found guilty of sheltering "riotous and abandoned company" should be fined.

Doubtless as a result of this and other incidents, March 1792 saw the following notice exhibited in Stornoway:

"Whereas many of the inhabitants of this place, feuars and others, sell by retail spirituous liquors, contrary to all regulation and order expressly made and given thereanent. Contributing to the utmost to debauch and corrupt the morals of the numerous lower class of people and to reduce their means and persons to poverty and want, Seaforth finds it absolutely necessary to put an entire stop to such abominable practices so ruinous to his estate and people. Therefore these are prohibiting and discharging all and every person in and about Stornoway, Knocknagour and Bayhead from selling, vending or retailing any spirituous liquors who have not a licence from Seaforth. With notification that all and every person who shall transgress shall be prosecuted there-for with the utmost vigour. Those licenced are desired and required to lodge information from time to time with Seaforth or his Factor against any contravening, that prosecution may be entered against them

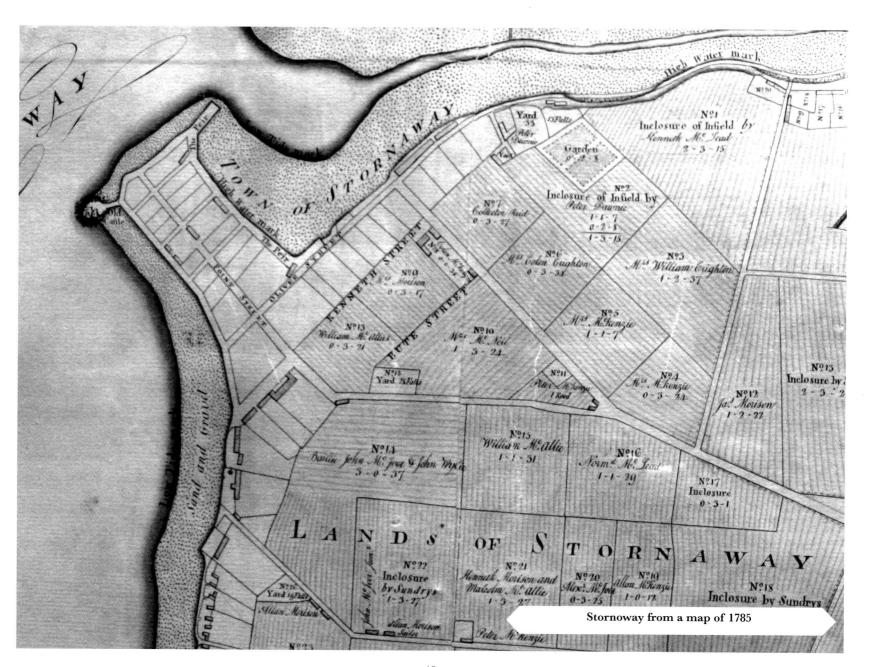

Stornoway from a map of 1785

and the vice entirely curbed and done away. It is also required that the feuars and others letting houses and lodgings do prevent and prohibit their lodgers from selling or retailing spirits, the feuars and others being responsible for the conduct and behaviour of those whom they take as tenants or to whom they let lodgings."

Compiled only a few years later, the Stornoway section of the First Statistical Account of Scotland notes that a "stoppage of the distilleries" had taken place recently meaning a tradition that "time out of remembrance" had been part of Stornoway life had had to cease. Until then, the mistress of the house provided the maidservants with a glass of whisky every morning; without it, there would be "discontent and idleness" throughout the day. Now it had been largely replaced with additional pay, although some families continued to provide the dram "to preserve peace and good order."

The church in Stornoway remained St Lennan's right in the centre of the town. John Downie took over as minister there on July 22, 1773, and the following June was writing to the Estate's Chamberlain (or Factor) referring to the need for repairs to his "dangerous and dilapidated" church. The Earl of Seaforth then decided it would be better to build a new church and asked the minister to prepare a plan and to recommend tradesmen to build it. In March 1787, Downie replied that the local tradesmen were "too poor, too ignorant and incapable of managing an affair of that magnitude." Downie moved to a new parish the following year long before work began on the church. Now known as St Columba's (Old) Parish Church, it was under construction by 1794, and was described in the First Statistical Account, a nationwide survey completed and published in 1799, as being 'new built and elegantly finished'.

The First Statistical Account also showed that Stornoway had grown greatly. There were now 35 vessels based in the harbour, and 4000 barrels of herring were being produced in good years. Export of cod was also having a national impact, records show. There were three schools in the town – the new ones being one created by the Society for Propagating Christian Knowledge and the other being a spinning school, created jointly by the Society and the Seaforths. The spinning school was spinning and knitting stockings and was working successfully in Stornoway although two other similar schemes in rural

Lewis had failed to attract enough participants. In the fields, potatoes had been added to the regular crops of oats and barley.

One writer in The First Statistical Account notes that the new-born babies in Lewis were afflicted by what is now known as infant tetanus, and has been specifically associated with St Kilda. The babies died of "convulsive fits" about the "fifth night after their birth" but the writer adds that this type of sickness has been reduced. Inoculation against smallpox was already being practiced in Stornoway as well, within a very short time after its discovery in England.

There was one new road, from Stornoway to Barvas, but roadbuilding had only begun in 1791, the Account states. There were 67 slated houses in the town – of which 26 had been built between 1784 and 1796 – as well as a Town House, the Customs House, and an Assembly Room. Along Bayhead there were around 20 thatched houses with strong walls and gables and glass windows. To the north of the town there were, the account states, "a great number of miserable thatched huts." Seaforth had built more new houses with gardens in what is now Newton and was encouraging people to take up the option of renting these houses.

In total, the population of the parish of Stornoway was 2639 in 1796, compared to an estimate of 1812 only 40 years earlier, a rise of 46 per cent.

Trades up in arms

In 1772 the following extraordinary coat was registered for the Incorporated Trades of Stornoway : Quarterly of ten; three, three, three, and one. The fields are all azure except numbers two and four, for the fields of which no tincture is assigned ; they are respectively charged with —

1, a hammer in pale, and in chief a crown proper, for the smiths ;

2, a pair of scissors expanded in saltire, their points in chief, for the tailors;

3, a leopard's head affronte proper, holding a shuttle in his mouth, argent, for the weavers;

4, a ship ready to be launched, proper, ensigned

with the colours of Scotland, for the ship-carpenters ;

5, a wright's square and a pair of compasses, their legs interlaced proper, for the wrights ;

6, an axe and adze in saltire proper, for the coopers

7, a cutting-knife erected, and in chief a coronet proper, for the shoemakers ;

8, a mason's square and a pair of compasses, their legs interlaced, argent, for the masons ;

9, a pair of large dressing-scissors, their points in chief, a little expanded, argent, for the dyers and dressers ;

10, a heckle argent, for the hecklers.

From THE ARMS OF THE BARONIAL AND POLICE BURGHS OF SCOTLAND

BY JOHN MARQUESS OF BUTE, K. T. ; J. H. STEVENSON; AND H. W. LONSDALE

Published in EDINBURGH by WILLIAM BLACKWOOD & SONS 1903

Town Hall shields

In 1891 a set of armorial bearings representing the coats of arms was presented to the Town by Dr. J. L. Robertson, H.M. Chief Inspector of Schools. The shields were manufactured by Messrs Hay & Lyalls of Edinburgh under Dr Robertson's supervision.

At the time that the coats of arms were registered, the only other Scottish town to have such bearings properly registered with the Lyon office was Aberdeen. In addition, anything with false arms and emblems displayed on it should be forfeit to the Crown.

Stornoway, in 1891, had no public building in which to display these emblems and, by agreement, they were hung in Lodge Fortrose for what became 14 years until the new Town Hall was completed.

At the opening of the new Town Hall on Wednesday 19th June 1928 a further two shields were mounted in the Hall. These are shown below , and are the clan crests of Thomas Basset Macaulay, who officially opened the new Hall, and John Bain of Chicago. Both made very generous donations to the cost of rebuilding.

See shields on Pages 25-26

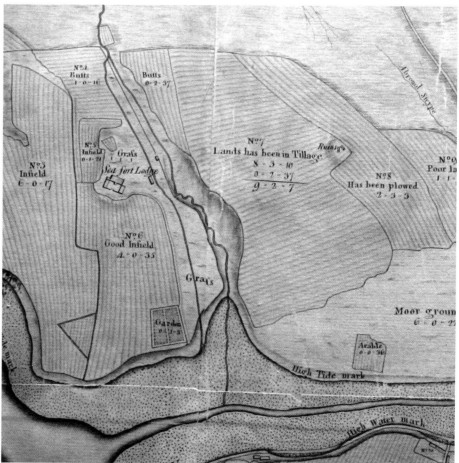

Some the walls of Seaforth Lodge survive within the structure of Lews Castle – part of a wall and window are seen left – while above is the layout of the Lodge in 1785 from a contemporary map

The picture above shows Carn House where it used to stand next to the Town Hall. This was the birthplace of Colonel Colin Mackenzie (1754 –1821) who became Surveyor General of India, and an internationally renowned art collector and orientalist. Mackenzie produced many of the first accurate maps of India, and his research and collections contributed significantly to the field of Asian studies.

A member of the Seaforth Mackenzie family which then owned the Isle of Lewis, he began his career as a customs officer in Stornoway, but at age 28, joined the British East India Company as an officer in the engineers. In 1799, he was part of the British force in the Battle of Seringapatam, where Tipu Sultan, Maharaja of Mysore was defeated by the British. He led the Mysore survey between 1800 and 1810. The survey was conducted by a massive team of draughtsmen and illustrators who collected material on the natural history, geography, architecture, history, customs,

and folk tales of the region. This created an unprecedented collection of material - including 2000 drawings and 8000 copies of inscriptions. He later spent two years in Java, part of the Dutch East Indies, when it was occupied by the British during the Napoleonic Wars and got as far as Bali where he spoke against slavery.

Mackenzie used his military career and salary to support his research into the history, religion, philosophy, ethnology, folklore, art, and mathematics of India and Java. He hired learned Brahmins to assist him with surveys and translations of manuscripts. Mackenzie researched Indian mathematics and India's system of logarithms after writing a biography of John Napier who discovered logarithms. Logarithms were vital to advanced mathematics and other sciences including navigation in the era before computers. Mackenzie never returned to the Western Isles and died in 1821 in Calcutta, India, where he is buried. Carn House was demolished in the 1950s.

Lazy Corner – seen right – is so-called because sea-borne rubbish used to accumulate in the corner of the quays and not move whatever the tide. It is watched over today, as it was 100 years ago, by the Town House. A cafe and restaurant in recent decades, a significant building on the same site is shown on a 1785 map of Stornoway. It may have been an early town Tolbooth and was later where the Town Council met. Its unusual angle to the street echoes the angle of the ditch dug by Cromwellian soldiers when they fortified the town in 1653 – and may therefore be, in origin, one of Stornoway's oldest buildings.

Freight and passenger traffic to the mainland grew continually over the decades. Pictured below right, the Clansman of David MacBrayne is seen alongside the original No 1 pier which was built to half its present length in wood in 1882, replacing a smaller steamer pier. If so, the image seems to have been taken before the Fish Mart was built in 1896.

Memories of past battles … at the time when work began on Lews Castle in 1847, three years after James Matheson bought Lewis from the Mackenzie family, only a fragment remained of Stornoway's original Castle. This ruin, destined to disappear under Number 1 Pier, had been the centre of much warfare in the era of the Macleod chiefs, ending in the early 1600s. It was mostly demolished at the time of the Cromwellian occupation in 1653 when the remaining stonework was used to build a citadel somewhere between the present Castle Street, orignally called Churchyard Lane before it was widened, and where Amity House now stands.

As demand for more English church services grew throughout the 19th Century, one major development came with the establishment of the Free English Church in 1875, to provide for English speaking residents and visitors who were adherents of the Free Church. They obtained a site for a new church the following year at the corner of Francis Street and Kenneth Street, and the Free English Church opened in October 1878. The church hall was built in 1890, and the spire erected in 1911 – so the picture on the right was taken well before that. Alexander Mackenzie, the first European to cross North America, was born in a house that stood on this site.

The congregation of the United Free English Church chose to change their name to Martin's Memorial Church of Scotland, in memory of their first minister, Donald Martin in 1929. That was when in Stornoway, as nationally, the United Free Church came together with the established church to form the Church of Scotland. At the same time, Stornoway's United Free High Church became the High Church of Scotland as it is today.

Tranquil scene – 100 years ago a fountain provided by the Matheson family – then the owners of Lewis – stood in an open area outside what was then the Post Office in Perceval Square, itself named after Sir James Matheson's wife's family.

The last years of the 19th century saw rapid expansion for Stornoway as the port's facilities grew to cope with the booming herring trade. Huge numbers of barrels accumulated every year on South Beach Quay for the Herring Girls to pack. The picture also shows some of the buildings on South Beach Street before the first Town Hall was built – so this is the scene as it was in the late 1890's. In the background is the former Waverley Hotel.

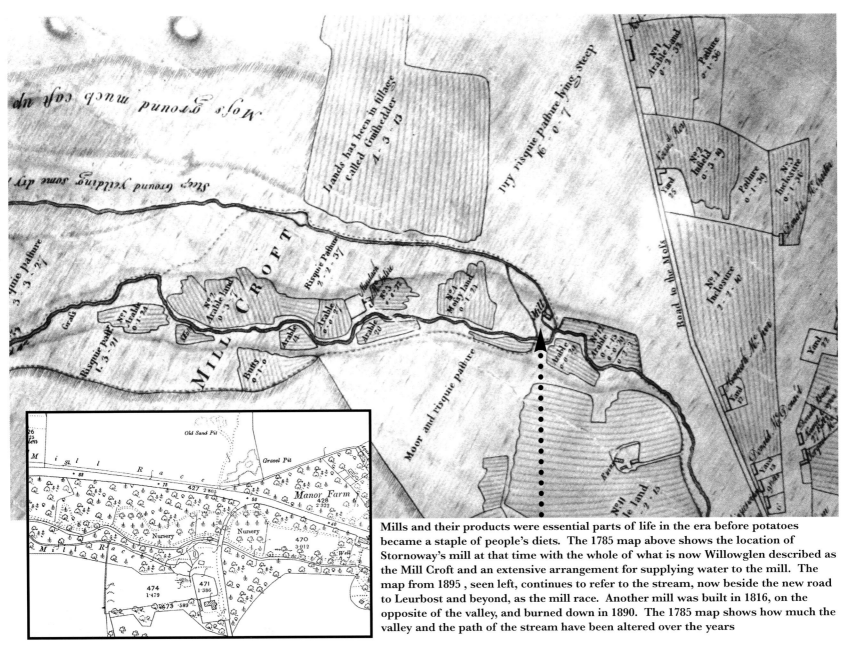

Mills and their products were essential parts of life in the era before potatoes became a staple of people's diets. The 1785 map above shows the location of Stornoway's mill at that time with the whole of what is now Willowglen described as the Mill Croft and an extensive arrangement for supplying water to the mill. The map from 1895 , seen left, continues to refer to the stream, now beside the new road to Leurbost and beyond, as the mill race. Another mill was built in 1816, on the opposite of the valley, and burned down in 1890. The 1785 map shows how much the valley and the path of the stream have been altered over the years

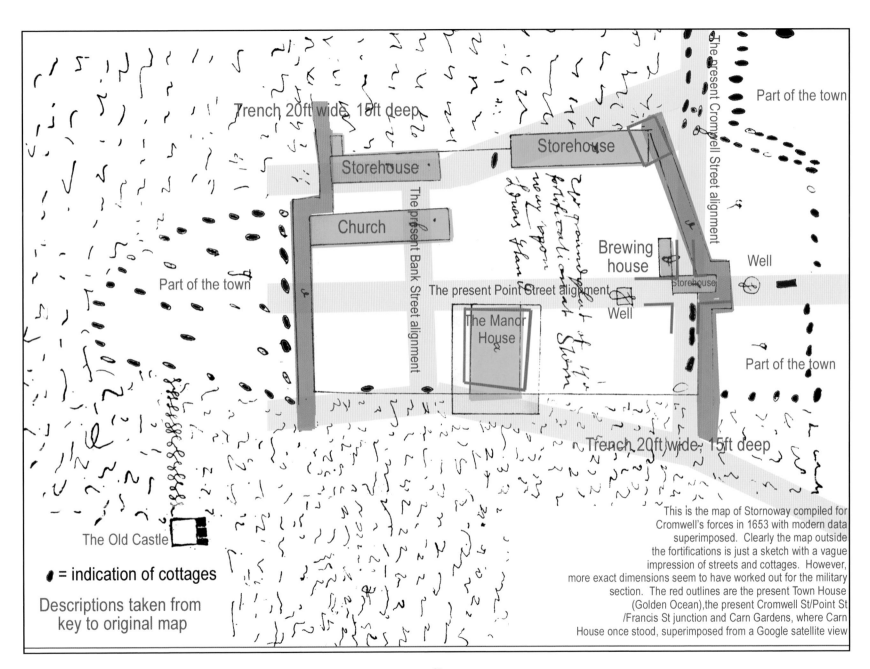

Trench 20ft wide, 15ft deep

Storehouse

Storehouse

The present Cromwell Street alignment

Part of the town

Church

The present Bank Street alignment

Brewing house

Well

Storehouse

Part of the town

The present Point Street alignment

Well

The Manor House

Part of the town

Trench 20ft wide, 15ft deep

The Old Castle

◗ = indication of cottages

Descriptions taken from key to original map

This is the map of Stornoway compiled for Cromwell's forces in 1653 with modern data superimposed. Clearly the map outside the fortifications is just a sketch with a vague impression of streets and cottages. However, more exact dimensions seem to have worked out for the military section. The red outlines are the present Town House (Golden Ocean), the present Cromwell St/Point St /Francis St junction and Carn Gardens, where Carn House once stood, superimposed from a Google satellite view

Smiths

Hecklers

Coopers

Tailors

Ship carpenters

Incorporated Trades
of Stornoway

Dyers

Armorial Bearings and Crests in the Town Hall

The photographs across these pages show the crests and bearings on display on the walls and above the stage and entrance doors of the Town Hall. In 1891 a set of armorial bearings was presented to the town by Dr J. L. Robertson, H. M. Chief Inspector of Schools. The shields were manufactured by Messrs Hay & Lyalls of Edinburgh under Dr Robertson's supervision.

At that time, the only other Scottish town to have such bearings properly registered with the Lyon office was Aberdeen. An article in the Aberdeen Free Press of 16th March 1891 stated: "It is a remarkable fact that in 1772 the crafts (incorporated presumably long before) of the remote and not over-opulent burgh of Stornoway would have had so much public spirit and appreciation of heraldic propriety as to apply to the Lyon Office for formal grants of arms." Although the Trades of Edinburgh, Glasgow, Dundee, Perth and Inverness were using 'emblems displayed on shields' they had no right to do so and, under Acts of Parliament of 1592 and 1672, were liable to be 'incarcerat in the narrest prison'.

Stornoway, in 1891, had no public building in which to display these emblems and, by agreement, they were hung in Lodge Fortrose for what became 14 years until the new Town Hall was completed. At the opening of the new Town Hall on Wednesday 19th June 1928 a further two shields were mounted in the Hall. These are all also shown left, and are the family crests of Thomas Basset Macaulay, who officially opened the new Hall, and John Bain of Chicago. Both made very generous donations to the cost of rebuilding.

The Incorporated Trades Society was formed by "merchants, shipowners, artisans, mariners, labourers and others, inhabitants of the town and vicinity of Stornoway." it was a mutual benefit society to support "sick and decayed members" and to cover funeral costs. Members had to be in the society for three years to claim any benefits. It is not known when it ceased to exist but it was flourishing in 1845, and changed some of its rules in 1856.

Shoemakers

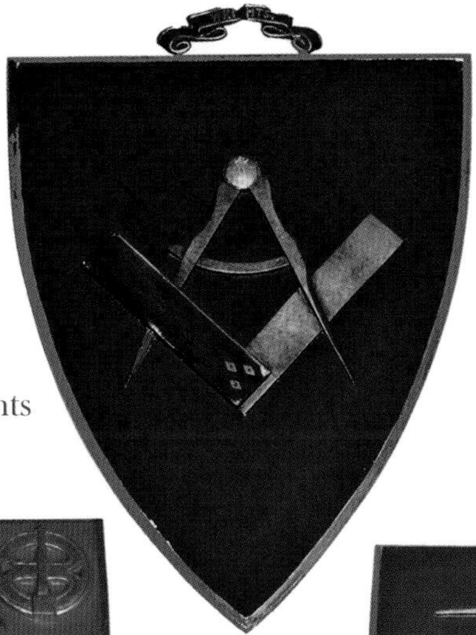

Wrights

The Macaulays

The Bain family emblem

Weavers

Masons

Local money

Stornoway had its own notes at a time – 1823 – when private issues were rarely considered but the Seaforth owners were facing a number of financial problems just as the national economy, after the Napoleonic Wars and before the Railway Age, was facing major challenges itself.

The man behind the notes was James Alexander Stewart (1784 – 1843), the grandson of the 6th Earl of Galloway, the nephew of the 7th Earl, and the son of Vice-Admiral Keith Stewart. On 21 May 1817 Stewart married Lady Hood, who was the widow of Admiral Sir Samuel Hood, and the eldest daughter of Francis Humberton Mackenzie, Lord Seaforth. When Stewart married Lady Hood he took his wife's family name, thus becoming James Alexander Stewart Mackenzie.

Lord Seaforth's four sons all died before him, and on his own death in 1815 the estate passed to his eldest daughter. At the time of Stewart Mackenzie's marriage to Lady Hood two years later, the Seaforth estate was in a bad way. In 1820 Stewart Mackenzie wrote to the Bank of Scotland seeking the establishment of a branch of that bank in Stornoway. In that correspondence he says that the kelp crop for the Seaforth estate was worth "£5000 to £7000 annually", as well as stating that the rents from tenanted land totalled "between £11000 & £12000".

Stewart Mackenzie no doubt believed that he could solve his situation with careful management and some help from the banks in the form of finance – but there was no bank at hand to provide the necessary loan. There had been a branch of the Aberdeen Commercial Bank on Lewis some time prior to 1820 with the Factor of the island as the agent, but at the death of the Factor the branch was "given up". The Greenock Bank sent an agent to attend the herring fleet when the season came, but it seems that their agent (and probably the bank) was not willing to provide a loan. The lack of a bank branch in Stornoway was the reason Stewart Mackenzie wrote the letter mentioned above to the Bank of Scotland in 1820.

His desire to attract the Bank of Scotland to Stornoway was almost certainly to use the branch facility as a convenient source of loans to himself, and in his letter he offers the services of his own employees to run the branch: "If the Branch were placed under the management of the Chamberlain & Factor of the Island with a confidential clerk sent from the Bank I should have no doubt of its success".

The front of the Mackenzie banknote

It was common knowledge that many of the Scottish banks provided a greater percentage of their loans to stockholders of the banks and to the banks' agents, rather than to the public – so Stewart Mackenzie felt that a branch under the tutelage of the Seaforth estate should be able to provide loans to the estate. The application to have a branch of the Bank of Scotland in Stornoway was rejected.

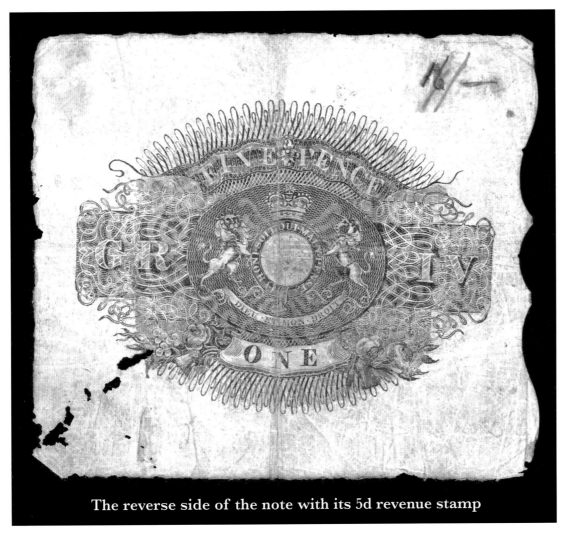

The reverse side of the note with its 5d revenue stamp

Around 1822 Stewart Mackenzie decided to issue his own notes perhaps in an effort to provide some relief from the estate's creditors. It's likely he planned to pay his workers and various creditors with his own notes instead of bank notes or coins. It was perfectly legal, as it was a common law right in Scotland at that time, for any person to issue their own notes, as long as the value of the notes was one pound or greater, the issuer had a licence to issue notes, and stamp duty was paid on the notes. He may also have been responding to the shortage of convertible currency in Scotland during the first few decades of the 19th century, which affected areas like the Hebrides more than elsewhere because of the lower levels of commercial activity.

It is uncertain how many notes were issued by Stewart Mackenzie, but it would seem to be less than a thousand. They were printed by "Rowe, 'Change Alley, London" on watermarked paper (the watermark being scrollwork around the border of the note), and carried a 5d revenue stamp on the reverse side of the note.

The vignette of the note shows a sailing ship without sails, but with a flag carrying "Flourish Commerce" flying from the jack mast. The ship, and an anchor lying on its side, sit above a panel containing the name of the town, shown as "STORNAWAY". Surprise has often been expressed at such an obvious "misspelling". However, many words of the 18th and 19th century are today spelled differently and there was greater variation then – Lewis was sometimes spelled not only "Lews" but also "Lewes".

The design includes the letters "JASM" (for James Alexander Stewart Mackenzie) in the centre, with two groups of four letters placed either side. To the left of "JASM" is "SSSS" (in different styles of the letter "S"), and to the right "MMMS", possibly referring to "Stewarts" and "Mackenzies".

The text of the note reads: "I Promise to pay on Demand to *the chamberlain of the Lewis* or Bearer One Pound Sterling at the Counting Room here." (The italics is handwritten.) The note is signed "J A Stewart Mackenzie", with the date and numbers being entered by hand.

The short life of the issue suggest the venture was not a success. By 1829 he was again making an application for the opening of a branch of a bank in Stornoway, this time to the National Bank of Scotland. This application was successful and an auxiliary branch of the National Bank was opened in June 1830.

Things still did not go smoothly, however. In 1835 Alexander Stewart the retiring Factor of Lewis, in a letter to Stewart Mackenzie, bemoans the fact that the bank agency was in the hands of Roderick Morison and L. McIver, who monopolised the fishing industry and the distilleries on Lewis. (Roderick Morison also acted for the Seaforth estate.)

In his letter Alexander Stewart proposed to seek the establishment of a branch of the Commercial Bank of Scotland in Stornaway with himself as agent, in an effort to right the wrongs he illustrated. However, minutes of the Commercial Bank show that the application was considered, but rejected.

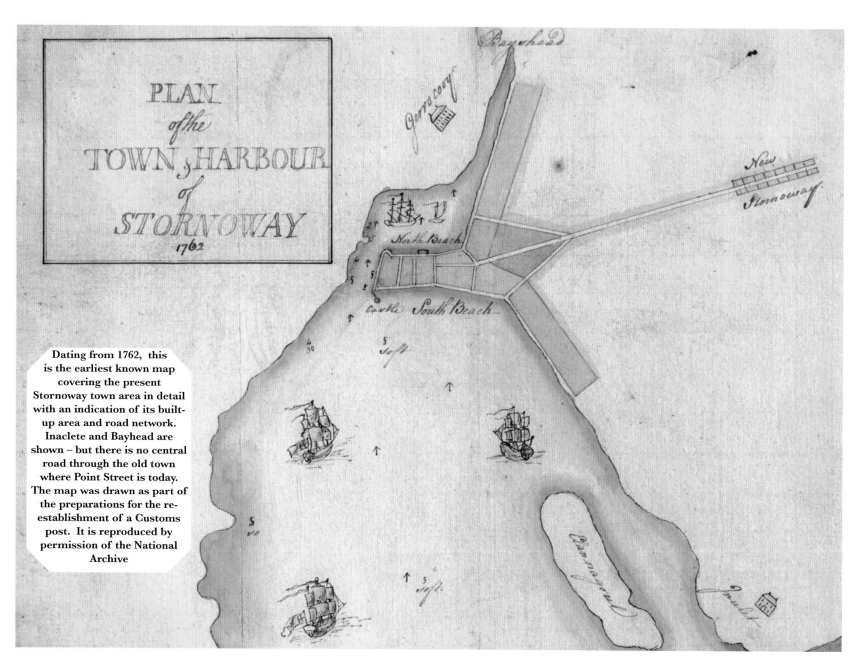

PLAN of the TOWN & HARBOUR of STORNOWAY 1762

Dating from 1762, this is the earliest known map covering the present Stornoway town area in detail with an indication of its built-up area and road network. Inaclete and Bayhead are shown – but there is no central road through the old town where Point Street is today. The map was drawn as part of the preparations for the re-establishment of a Customs post. It is reproduced by permission of the National Archive

This painting of "The village of Stornoway and shooting lodge on the Isle of Lews" completed in 1798 by James Barret was bought by Comhairle nan Eilean Siar, with help from the National Art Collection Fund (Art Fund); the National Fund for Acquisitions administered by the National Museums of Scotland ; and the Lewis Museum Trust. The picture was conserved with the help of public donations – conservators removed over-painting added since the work was originally completed. The artist seems to have been painting from Gallows Hill but the extension of woodland over the years makes it impossible to replicate this view exactly. Clearly shown is Seaforth Lodge which preceded Lews Castle; the remains of Stornoway Castle in the harbour; the density of settlement around the harbour; and the recently finished parish church of St Columba, right.

William Daniel's view of Stornoway in 1819. The houses along what is now Cromwell Street appear to be stylised rather than accurate representations of the buildings of that era. This is one of a series of illustrations by Daniell, published as 'A voyage round the north and north-west Coast of Scotland and the adjacent islands with a series of views illustrative of their character and most prominent features'. Daniell was a landscape-painter and in 1814 he began his 'Voyage round Great Britain', published in four volumes in 1825.

A miscellany of Stornoway I

■ In 4,000 BC Gallows Hill (Cnoc na Croich) was the site of a chambered burial cairn. It is found at the highest point in the Lews Castle Grounds, from which you can look out over Stornoway. At this point it was not known as Gallows Hill – it was not until the 1600s, when the Mackenzies of Kintail owned Lewis, that it was named this. Lord Kintail was the man to raise the gallows on the hill, in order to hang the wrongdoers of the island. During the early years of World War II, when invasion was imminent, Gallows Hill was also one of the places throughout Britain where a secret bunker was built: – it had a locked metal door and was concealed by bushes. This was part of Prime Minister Winston Churchill's secret resistance army – the Auxiliaries – who were to fight on as guerillas against the Nazi forces if an invasion came.

■ The Statistical Account of Scotland, published in 1799, says that in Stornoway "good houses are let at from £15 to £25 per annum, and rooms and lesser dwellings in like proportion." The rents were higher than on the mainland because even then, the writer states, "the houses are built at considerable cost, because all the materials are imported, the stones not excepted." The schoolmaster at the parochial school was paid £25 a year and his assistant £15. At the SPCK school, the salaries were £17 and £8. The quarter fees for pupils also varied; for instance, navigation cost 10s [there were 20 shillings in a £ then] at the SPCK school but £1 1s at the parochial school. Book-keeping was 5s a quarter at the SPCK school but 10s 6d at the parochial school. Other courses included Latin, arithmetic, English, writing, and geography. Meanwhile sub-tenants of the tacksmen paid between £1 10s and £3 a year in rent and had to provide 12 days of service. Work on the herring busses – large fishing boats which were the core of the herring fishery – paid £1 a month. Workers in the kelp industry earned £1 10s per ton of tangle collected. Road workmen were paid 8d (eight old pence - there were 240 in a £) a day. They were paid 6d a day if they were also getting two meals and a dram. Women got 6d a day or 4d with two meals and a dram. The day wages of a carpenter,

joiner or mason were 1s 6d with meals. Shoemakers earned between 10d and 1s a day. [By comparison, the labourers employed building the Forth and Clyde Canal across Central Scotland that was completed in 1790 were paid 10d a day.] Potatoes sold at 3 to 5s a barrel. Beef was sold at 1½d to 3d a lb. Butter was 12s and 14s a stone [about 1s/lb or roughly 5p for 500 grammes - allowing for historic inflation, that is £4.30 in modern money.] By contrast an entire chicken cost only 6d [half a shilling]; pork was 2d/lb; while sheep were 3s to 4/6d each.

■ Population growth was incredibly rapid between 1750 and 1850. According to the First Statistical Account, of 1799, the population of the parish of Stornoway was 2639 in 1796, up by 827 or 45 per cent since 1755. The rapidly rising local population is also suggested by another figure. In 1792, there were 135 baptisms but only 20 burials. The Second Statistical Account of Scotland, compiled in the mid 1830s, shows the population of the parish of Stornoway had more than doubled in just over 30 years, from 2639 in 1796, to 5491 in 1831. Almost 50 per cent, 2372, were under 15 years of age. By the 1830s there were 13 schools in the parish of Stornoway, including two run by the Gaelic School Society and one each in Knock and Melbost.

■ The Broadbay flounder was said to be "the finest in the world," according to the The Second Statistical Account of Scotland (1833). Hake, haddock sole, conger eels along with whales, killer whales or other dolphins and porpoises also formed part of the diet. Haddocks were sold at 1s a dozen.

■ Stornoway had around 2500 inhabitants by 1867. At that time. its streets were lit by gaslight. Mail was taken from Ullapool to Stornoway five times a week in summer and three times a week in winter. The old castle remained visible in the harbour, with the wall of the keep still reaching 20ft in height..

■ The Pentland Road which runs across the moors between Carloway and the Marybank district of Stornoway, along with a branch to Breasclete Pier, was originally

conceived as a railway, with several miles of the roadbeds at each end of the route constructed to rail standards. The survey of the route was paid for by the Western Highlands and Islands Commission of 1890. In its report the Commission noted there was no one in the Island prepared to run the proposed railway, let alone contribute to the cost of construction. The Government was expected to both pay for it and run it, the Commission commented sourly, regretting the lack of "local initiative". Survey plans show the proposed line would have swept over the Laxdale Road on a viaduct on its way to a terminus on South Beach. As late as 1912, when the road was finally opened about 16 years after the work began, there were pleas for a rail line to be built along it. No work was ever done on the route between Lochs Road in Marybank and the town.

■ Remains of other narrow gauge railway lines built in the Lord Leverhulme era after 1918 are visible in various places between Cannery Road, Stornoway and the Braighe, and by the Stornoway War Memorial. These routes which brought sand and quarry stone to construction projects in the town were in use for less than five years. Until recent years islanders could recall the thrill of hitching lifts on the slow-moving freight trains. In the 1860s about three and half miles of tramways were laid as a network to bring peat to the Lewis Chemical Works at Marybank. The trackbeds remain visible as do similar trackbeds at Garrabost where an oil refinery and the brickworks were established. In the 1930s a narrow gauge railway was built to link the Stornoway Water Works with Loch Mòr an Stairr to assist construction of the dam.

■ The Rev Colin Mackenzie, writing in 1796, after being a minister in Stornoway since 1789, describes the weather on Lewis as follows: "The seasons and weather are very variable and not to be depended on. We have little warmth or heat in summer; autumn is rainy; the winter not so severe as usual on the continent [the mainland] but more open and free of snow and frost. Our spring is often wet and cold."

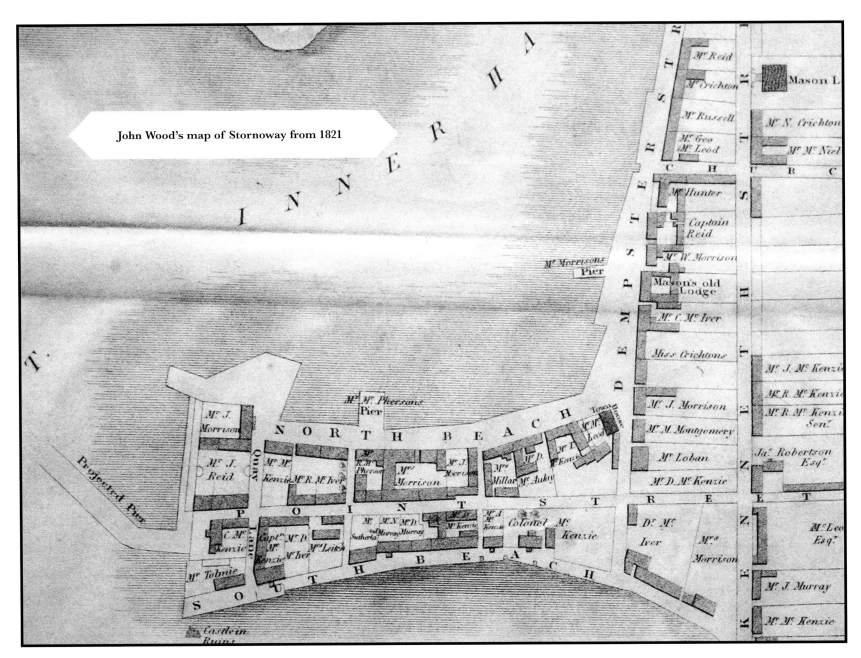

John Wood's map of Stornoway from 1821

34

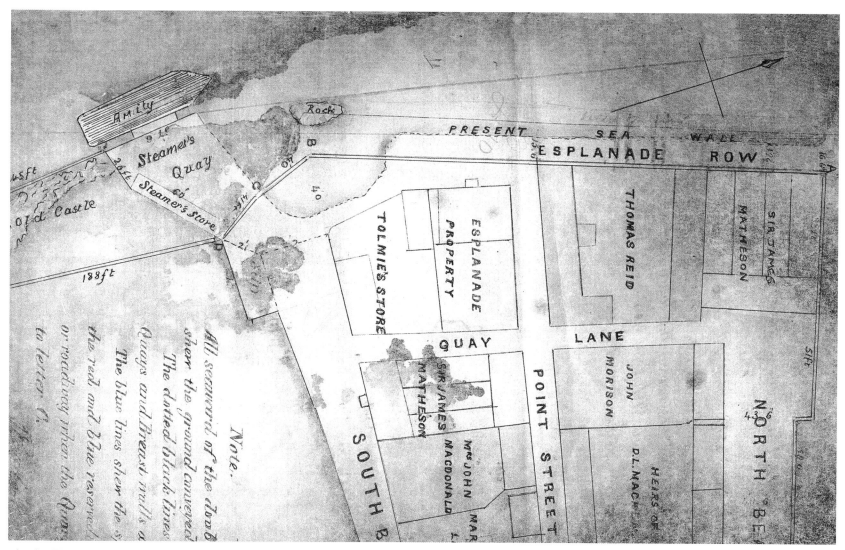

Amity House, the headquarters of the Stornoway Port Authority (formerly the Stornoway Pier and Harbour Commission) was so named in September 1962 after the barge Amity, a derelict sailing ship that had been used as a landing stage in the early days of Sir James Matheson's ownership of Lewis. The location of Amity by the first steamer pier can be seen in this map from 1851. Amity House was formerly the Old Custom House but in 1962 the new Custom House was built and to avoid confusion, the older building was renamed. The map, property of the SPA, was saved from the Town Hall fire of 1918 and still shows the marks of the blaze.

Catching whales in Stornoway harbour

The only association between whaling and Stornoway recalled in modern times is that involving seamen who went to the South Atlantic hunting for whales in the mid decades of the 20th century.

However as late as 1882, traditional inshore whale-catching of the sort that is now solely associated with the Faroe Isles, was taking place in Stornoway Bay, involving a vast number out of the local population in an impromptu slaughter. Similar hunts took place all across the Nordic region of Scotland – in Orkney, Shetland and Caithness as well as Lewis.

Whales had been plentiful – and hunted – for many centuries in these areas, although not further south where the Norse traditions were weaker. For instance, Dean Donald Munro said in his "A Description of the Western Isles of Scotland", compiled in 1549 there was "A grait take of quhailles is oftimes in this countrey, so that be the relatione of the maist ancient in this countrey, ther comes 26 or 27 quhailles young and ald to the teynd anes ther." This indicates that a tithe (or tenth) portion was 26 or 27 so the total size of the groups of whales driven ashore was usually around 260/270.

In the next century, Captain John Dymes, writing in 1630, said that "This last yeare there came in great stoare of young Whales into one of theire Loughes which the inhabitants inclosed with boates, and killd more then one hundred of them with their swords and theire bowes and arrowes, for want of better engines, and made meat of them all, and for want of salt to save it they tooke the sea oare (ware) and burned it and then powderd it with the ashes thereof, which afterwards beinge dryed in the smoake they eate it like bacon."

Writing in 1695, Martin Martin said that the fishing around Carloway was regularly disrupted by whales. He was told that about 15 years previously a whale had overturned a fishing boat and devoured three of the crew. On the east side of Lewis there were "many whales of different sizes" in the herring bays."The natives imploy many boats together in pursuit of the whales, chasing them up into the bays till they wound one mortally, and then it runs ashore and they say that all the rest commonly follow the tract of its blood and run themselves also on the shore in like manner; by which means many of them are killed. About five years ago there were fifty young whales kill'd in this manner and most of them eaten by the common people, who by experience find them very nourishing food; this I have been assur'd of by several persones, but particularly by some poor meagre people who become plump and juicy by this food in the space of a week; they call it Sea Pork, for so it signifies in their language." Apparently, the meat of bigger whales had more of a "purgative" effect than that from smaller animals.

Dr John Mackenzie, in the book A Hundred Years in the Highlands written by his nephew Osgood, records a whale hunt in Stornoway harbour in about 1820. He recalls:" From Stornoway pier the long harbour was visible down to the open sea about three miles. Soon after dawn on a calm, grey morning, almost everyone (many half-dressed and hatless) [scampered] away up the town like mad bulls, roaring their loudest for all hands to get out the boats…every male… seemed gone crazy, shouting out Mucan mara, mucan mara (Whales! Whales!)

"They… tumbled into the many boats at the pier and on the shore, first throwing into them heaps of smallish stones, evidently to be used as round shot for the enemy. A line of six or eight boats were acting in concert with the harbour boats, some of the men rowing and others standing up on the thwarts and waving hats and jackets to indicate something not yet visible to us landlubbers.

"In a few minutes some thirty boats were steering down the harbour close to the land on out side, rowing as if for dear life…we saw them very soon pass the eight boats at the harbour mouth, which, it seemed, had gone off early to their ordinary long line fishings, when they fell in with a great school of whales that were capering about like lunatics in the sea. The moment the supporting boats passed those which had discovered the whales, we saw them wheel round outside them from the shore, and soon a regular barrier of boats was formed quite across the bay at about one hundred yards beyond the original fishermen, who then left their stations to join the new flotilla

"Meanwhile another line of boats, arriving later, formed a second barrier one hundred yards or so nearer the ocean than the first one… the crews of the boat were waving coats and throwing stones vigorously at the coveted mammals, and the sea was boiling with the capers of the monsters, who were growing alarmed at their danger.

"The whales dived under the first line of boats and back out to sea. But all is not over, for the fugitives have taken fright at the second line of boats, and the first line has divided in the middle passed farther out in two columns, to reform their line again beyond the second.

"This game went on for rather longer that the fishers desired, for the demands upon wind and limb were severe, and they had started early, without food or liquor, their only breakfast being deferred hope, which does not take long to digest. However, about noon the whales seemed to have had long enough of men and boats, and their leader … steered up the harbour and was soon nearly opposite the town.

"All was most quiet and silent there, lest any noise on shore might frighten the whales out to sea again. The harbour grows so much narrower near the town that the boats come gradually closer together, and showers of stones were thrown at every whale who showed above water."

From what happens next it seems that the earlier understanding about shooting the leader and the rest of the school following him ashore had been lost. Dr Mackenzie says: "I fetched my double rifle and its ammunition from the hotel, and became so excited that when the leading whale raised its head high enough to show his eye, I fired without asking anyone's leave, feeling certain I would extinguish it.

"A universal groan and unmistakable bad language from land and sea rather shocked me for a moment; but I am certain the shot was a wise one, for the leader, instead of turning away to sea as my groaners were sure he would do, quietly continued his course up the harbour till he grounded.

"It was high water or nearly so, and ninety-five others of his large followers ran ashore also or hung about him like a swarm of bees round their queen, though there was nothing to prevent all of them going back to sea if they had resolved to so. As soon as those in the boats knew that the lead whale was grounded, the boats dashed in among the shoal, busy with every deadly weapon they could lay their hands on, till the sea was mere bloody mud.

"Weapons included oars and guns, boat-hooks, old broad-swords, and other kinds of lethal weapons, one of them even bearing a kitchen spit with its wooden wheels at the end like a gallant lancer's spear." Mackenzie saw the spit-bearer poking his spit into shining backs as they emerged from the water alongside his boat. As for himself, he kept popping away at point-blank range with his double rifle until he had used up all his bullets.

Every now and then a boat was overturned by a whale rising beneath it; the noise of semi-drowning people, hunters, whales and onlookers was astounding; and everyone worked busily to make sure that there was no risk of any of the whales swimming out to sea again at the next high tide. One boat struck near the shore, and the badly wounded whale took to spouting blood in a stream as thick as Mackenzie's arm from his blow-hole. From astern of the stranded boat, the whale rather astonished the crew by regularly deluging them with a stream of pure blood.

The whales "were of all sizes, most of them about twenty to twenty-four feet long [6.1-7.3 m], but some were down to four feet [1.2 m] and in several places in the mud I could have taken up bowls of milk that had run out of the mother whales." Dr Mackenzie recalled that one of the whales spat out an 8/9lb salmon as fresh as if taken out of a net "evidently a salmon that intended to go up the river Creed, but had fallen in with a school of whales as they passed along!"

In April 1832, the Inverness Courier reported that an "immense school of whales" had appeared off Stornoway. "They were driven ashore by a troop of boats which put out from the harbour. Ninety-eight whales, some of them very large, were sold by public roup." The same newspaper reported in July 1844 that a large school of whales had been driven into a bay near Stornoway. The total number of whales killed was 179. Published in 1833, the Second Statistical Account states that it was a regular event for

Detail from a painting presented to Lodge Fortrose by Estate Factor Donald Munro on July 2, 1869. He said it showed "the capture of whales in Stornoway several years ago"

whales and other mammals to be driven ashore in groups of up to 150 by the inshore fishermen in their light boats.

Further similar hunts occurred in Stornoway in 1869 and 1882 but by the end of the century this tradition of occasional whaling was dying out all over Scotland and the 1882 hunt is the last recorded for Stornoway, although one occurred in Loch Erisort as late as 1934. However, a report of the 1869 hunt involving 185 whales suggests that the tradition was still strong then.

"Everybody who could get a boat joined in the chase. It lasted from midday to about seven o'clock in the evening.

Again and again, the whales made for the mouth of the harbour and it was feared they might escape. By persistent effort and never-tiring, the boats and boatmen at last got them into the inner harbour." Once again every available item was pressed into duty as a weapon – harpoons, grapes [hooks], knives and axes were all involved. The whales "swirled round and dashed their tails madly splashing and wetting with blood and brine all who came near." Clearly it was a clear summer's night as the last whales were not dispatched until midnight. The whales were sold by auction again, realising between £300 and £400. The catch in 1844 had been sold for £483.

South Beach to North Beach – the old town crammed with history

In the great days of the herring fishery, South Beach quay was lined end to end with curing stations, herring girls hard at work gutting and packing the fish and vast piles of barrels.

South Beach was formerly a gently shelving beach on which boats were drawn up. In 1786, John Knox of the British Fisheries Society was very disappointed to see that the town had no proper quay and that the beaches were still in use for loading and unloading by means of lighters. North Beach on the other side of the old town was the same. Both North Beach and South Beach were largely infilled and a quayside wall built by the 1890s. The wharves were further extended in 1926. After the construction of the modern ferry terminal in the early 1990s, only part of one beach remains visible, at the far end of South Beach, next to No. 1 pier.

South Beach Street now starts with the headquarters of the Western Isles NHS Board. This was built in 1962 as the local office of Ross and Cromarty County Council that ran Lewis before local government reorganisation in 1975. This building stands on the site of an 18th century house, similar to that occupied by Tighean Innse Gall further along the street. At the back of the building is one of the town's wells, called Cromwell's Well, and said to be related to the Cromwellian fort of the mid 1650s. However, it seems likely this is a later misunderstanding. The only surviving map of the fort suggests there was a well somewhere around the site of the present Town Hall and another just outside the fort next to what is now Francis Street.

Further along South Beach is the British Legion building – housed in the former Stornoway Playhouse cinema which opened its doors for the first time in January 1934 and finally closed for good as a cinema in 1979. This stands on the site, until 1875, of the lawyers office of Donald Munro, notorious for his role as factor for Sir James Matheson. Munro, from Tain, was accepted to practice law in Stornoway in 1841 as Procurator-Fiscal. Ten years later he was joined by his cousin William Ross and they later became joint fiscals as well as controlling the only private legal practice in Lewis. One of the employees at Donald Munro's practice in its early years was Robertson Macaulay, whose father was from Uig and who later emigrated to Canada and became the driving force behind Sun Life Assurance.

His entry in the Canadian Dictionary of National Biography states: "He began work at age 12 as a construction labourer at Stornoway, Scotland. Possessing only the rudiments of education but imbued with the Scottish penchant for self-improvement, he devoted his evenings to unremitting study, concentrating on mathematics. He promptly secured an apprenticeship to the local solicitor and procurator fiscal. Macaulay's foray into law awakened his social conscience. As an officer of the court, he was obliged to evict crofters. The experience convinced him that economic security was the bedrock on which the well-being of families rested. The death of his father in 1847, when he was 14, cruelly reinforced this idea." Robertson Macaulay went on to revolutionise the insurance industry by putting customer satisfaction as a top priority.

An Lanntair now stands where there was a car park and for the younger generations these are the only two things that they've ever known to be there. But the land beneath the arts centre has an interesting past. In the 1890s, the building that was to be become the Imperial Hotel was built. It was on the hotel that the ropes were tied in order to help construct the spire of Martin's Memorial Church which prompted a local to say: "This was the first time that salvation has been tied to damnation".

The Imperial Hotel was also used as the headquarters for the Royal Naval Reserve from 1914 to 1919. Subsequently, in 1922, the Carnegie Trust sold the building to the Education Authority who could not afford to build a school hostel. This then became the Louise Carnegie hostel, the first school hostel in Ross and Cromarty. In 1972, new accommodation was found for the girls of the hostel, and the building was temporarily used by the Western Isles Regional Authority. In 1981, following the authority's relocation, when the Comhairle nan Eilean Siar headquarters was built, the building was then demolished, becoming the car park which existed until the Arts Centre was finally built there, opening in 2005.

As you walk towards the Town Hall along South Beach, the area of town to the right stretching across to the Inner Harbour was in 1654 the scene of what was one of the biggest land battles fought on Lewis, at least since the days of the Vikings. Hundreds of Islanders, led by Island chief Kenneth "Mor" Mackenzie, Earl of Seaforth, assaulted the Cromwellian fort and the town immediately in front of it in a surprise attack. Houses were left blazing, 12 of the English soldiers were killed, but the fort, with deep ditches running right across the peninsula of old Stornoway, defied the raiders. In the aftermath of the battle, the Cromwellian soldiers allied with members of the Macleod clan and slaughtered many supporters of the Mackenzies.

At the Cromwell Street junction, is the Thorlee Guesthouse, formerly the Waverley Hotel, with roofline busts of figures which may be related to Sir Walter Scot's Waverley series of novels; and opposite is the Town Hall, built originally in 1905, burned out in 1919 with the loss of many historical and irreplaceable records. It was rebuilt in the 1920s to be reopened in 1928 after funding came from exiles in the US and Canada.

In Carn Gardens, next to the Town Hall, a plaque commemorates Sir Colin Mackenzie, the first Surveyor-General of India who lived in Carn House on this site and died in Calcutta in 1821. In the first known plan of the

In a photograph taken between 1905 and 1914, South Beach is resplendent... the original Town Hall towers over the street and the Imperial Hotel dominates the Kenneth Street corner. Surviving records suggest there was a family home on part of the site from 1829. Then there seems to have been a problem with the ownership documents and Lady Matheson issued a charter of novodamus to the owners in 1884 to clarify their rights. The hotel was probably built after that and sold for £7,000 in 1897 (at least £690,000 in 2009 money) – but seems to have hit hard times after that and was converted into the Louise Carnegie Hostel for Girls in the 1920s.

centre of Stornoway, created by a Cromwellian officer in 1653, this seems to be the site of what was described as the Manor House, the most important domestic building in the town at the time.

The late 19th century saw extensive construction work – including the Old Bank of Scotland building, formerly the Caledonian Bank. The Star Inn, built around 1800, became the Lewis Coffee House about 1885, as pressure built up to reduce the level of drinking. This closed around 1915 and after the First World War came Lewis's own Prohibition era. For about five years from 1920-1925 Lewis was "dry". Only the Lewis Hotel where the bar first opened in 1820 still supplied beer under a legal loophole that allowed it to sell it in bulk. The contemporary visitors book of the Harris Hotel, Tarbert, outside the dry area, suggests that a journey south became additionally attractive for some of those who had access to motor vehicles at the time.

Continuing along South Beach, Castle Street, now a wide main road, was until the 1950s a narrow cross way like tiny Bank Street. Castle Street roughly marks the western end of the Cromwellian fort. Beyond, towards Esplanade Quay, there stood a defensive tower built by the occupying forces. The foundations of a major structure have been found there. The name Esplanade, an unusual word that originally meant a flat area outside a fortress, may date from that era. Along the seafront the Caledonian Hotel, was rebuilt after a destructive fire in 1962.

Facing out across the mouth of the inner harbour, Amity House, the headquarters of the Stornoway port authority, was built around 1830 and served as the Customs House for many years . It was named Amity House (after the hulk of the barque Amity which was moored nearby to form a quay in the 19th century) when it became the headquarters of the Stornoway Pier and Harbour Commission (now the Stornoway Port Authority) in 1978.

Beneath the Number 1 pier at the end of South Beach lie the remains of Stornoway's medieval castle. Built on an offshore rock, or skerry, like Kisimul Castle in Barra, a 12ft high section of wall, several feet thick survived until 1882. Stornoway Castle was largely demolished during the Cromwellian invasion in the 1650s. No. 1 pier was built to half its present length in wood in 1882, replacing an earlier smaller steamer pier. It was replaced with concrete in 1938 and further extended in 1947. Until demolition in 2007,

The original fish mart – its drinking fountain can be found in the new ferry terminal which mimics its shape

Number1 Pier was the site of the art deco style Maritime Buildings, built in 1935, which shared this architectural style with the former cinema and the James Street building that was formerly the offices of Newall's mill. A decorative plaque on the Maritime Buildings which explained the pier's location over the ruins of Stornoway Castle, is now in storage.

The original fishmart opened for business in 1894 on a site which is part of the car park near the old linkspan. Built at a cost of £1,200, the upper floor was designed to accommodate in a total of 14 offices. In May of 1894, the Fish Mart was officially opened by a Mr. Thomson, auctioneer, from Buckie. A handsome, double-faced clock, procured by public subscription, was presented to the Pier & Harbour Commission in July 1895 and, in September of that year, Angus MacRitchie, lamplighter, was offered the salary of 10s 6d per year to attend to its winding. In 1939, the Mart was scheduled for demolition, but due to a lack of funds, the Commission delayed the work and it was the early 1970s before the final decision was taken to demolish the building to prepare for the arrival of the first car ferries.

Some of the oldest surviving buildings in Stornoway are in the area between Amity House and North Beach Street, including the Sail Loft dating from around 1830. This is a key site in the history of Stornoway. Little was known about the history of these buildings until a feasibility study was done by the Highland Buildings Preservation Trust in 2002.

It was then established that the 18th century Customs House survives in the core of the building. Although it was remodelled in the nineteenth century, the original salt cellar from the Customs House, which was accessed from the gable facing onto the harbourside, still survives beneath the former Commercial Hotel. The north gable of the earlier structure, shown in an engraving from 1789, survives in the attic of the building which was reconstructed in 1822 as a merchant/fish curer's house and became a hotel at the end of the 19th century. The buildings at 6-8 North Beach are among the last remnants of the 18th Century town although more survives within the walls of the Lewis Hotel, extended in 1829.

Across Castle Street, the buildings now occupied by the Crown Hotel and the Pointers Youth Centre stand on the western part of the site of St Lennan's Church, built by Colin Mackenzie, first Earl of Seaforth and the first non-Macleod chief. Only the bell, of Dutch origin and dated 1631, survives and it is now installed in St Peter's Episcopal Church in Francis Street. Remains of burials have been dug up in the area around the Crown Hotel and in Castle Street, suggesting this was the site of the church's graveyard. St Lennan is an obscure patron saint for a church and this suggests that an earlier religious building may have existed on the site. It is possibly relevant that one origin for the name MacLennan in Gaelic is Mac Gille Fhinnein meaning the son of the follower of St Finnan. Born in Ireland and dying in 661, Finnan trained as a monk on Iona. He succeeded Saint Aidan as Bishop of Lindisfarne and leader of the Northumbrian church.

On the corner of South Beach and Cromwell Street, the Town House which is on the site of an earlier building dating back to the 1650s, overlooks Perceval Square, named after the family name of Sir James Matheson's wife, which only became a car park in recent years. Also overlooking it is Leverhulme House, which was the town Post Office 100 years ago, and is now the headquarters of the Stornoway Trust. (The Trust has, since 1923, been the elected landowner of Stornoway and the Broadbay area of Lewis after accepting the gift of the area from landowner Lord Leverhulme.)

Many shops were established in the mid-19th century in the town – the longest lasting being Charles Morrison's, an ironmongers, which opened in 1864 in Point Street and closed for good in 2002.

This is taken from the Illustrated London News of June 12, 1852. In an article accompanying the illustration, Lewis is described as having a population of 19,694 according to the previous year's census. The article makes clear that many of the innovations brought in by Sir James Matheson had already taken place, including the woods of the Castle Grounds, the building of the Castle, and the development of new roadways, bridges, drainage projects, and the Patent Slip ship building and repair yard that occupied land now taken up by a supermarket and car park.

The view above, taken from Cnoc Murchaidh Uilleam, is of the old Market Stance, probably around 1905. Latha na Drobh – the annual market day – was traditionally held on the second Wednesday of July near Beinn na Drobh (hence Bennadrove).

The actual site shown in the photograph is where the Gleann Seileach technology park now stands – the gateway into it, and formerly to the County Hospital was the gateway to the old Market Stance.

In 1920, the top or northern part of the site was feued to the Scottish Branch of the British Red Cross Society as a sanatorium for the soldiers and sailors hurt in the Great War.

As the County Hospital, it became a tuberculosis sanatorium and then a geriatric hospital. It was replaced by Ospadal nan Eilean in 1992.

Back in 1833, the "annual tryst or cattle-market" was a massive affair. The Second Statistical Accounts records that a square mile of moor was enclosed for the sale. " Several thousand head of cattle are exposed for sale, and two thousand at least change owners, in two days." At that time 20 or 30 drovers came from the mainland and "some from England."

The market was always held on the second Wednesday of July and the mailboat waited to bring purchasers across the Minch.

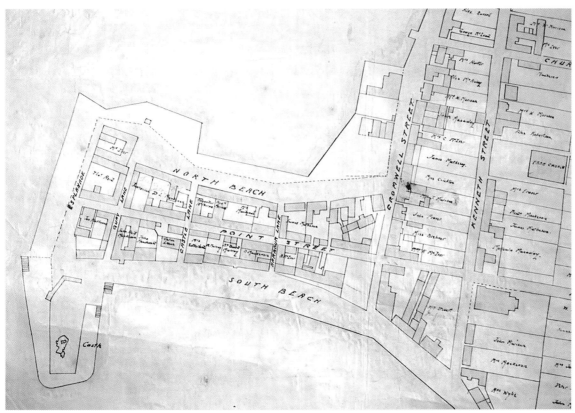

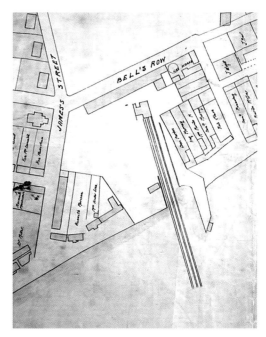

Above is a view of central Stornoway in 1880 and the Patent Slip at the same era. Below is the scene in 1931-2 on North Beach when the piling that covered the original beach was removed and infilled.

The picture above includes a view of the original Caledonian Hotel, destroyed in a tragic blaze on Sunday October 30th, 1966. In January 1901, the Town Council passed plans for "handsome new hotel proposed to be erected on South Beach" (Highland News, January 26, 1901). The original hotel was opened in 1902. The new building was put up in 1970.

The house to the left of the hotel, No 4, was the home in the 1950s of Donald Macleod, the father of two famous pipers, Pipe Major Donald Macleod MBE and Angus Macleod. The house was demolished in 1961 to provide accommodation for Stornoway Pier & Harbour Commission and the Customs & Excise.

To the right of the Caley is No 7 – Tigh na Cloinne – which was occupied in 1930 by Angus "The Caley" Macdonald who took the photograph. This building was demolished in 1957. It adjoins Churchyard Lane which, along with the houses to the right, was obliterated to create Castle Street in 1956. Churchyard Lane appears to contain a memory of the location of the original churchyard and burial ground for the first known church in Stornoway, St Lennan's, built around 1630 and in use until the end of the 18th Century. Construction work in this area of the town has revealed over the years various artefacts of human bones as archaeological evidence. St Lennan's was replaced when Lord Seaforth commissioned a new church, at the corner of what are now Lewis Street and Church Street, now known as St Columba's (Old) Parish Church.

In the 19th and early 20th centuries, herring dominated the town. Top left, Herring girls at work on Esplanade Quay. (A picture from the Joseph Cook Collection in Inverness Museum. © Highland Council (Inverness Museum) Licensor www.scran.co.uk) The others pictures are from earlier years – clockwise, Cromwell Street Quay, North Beach; and South Beach (where the bus station now is) with the curing and cooperage yard of James Flett & Co in the background.

From the Stornoway Trust archive - a record book dating back to the Mackenzie era and recording grants of a feu charter on August 30, 1823 (above) and August 30, 1825 (right)

Growth in home-ownership

The granting of feus for homes and businesses in the early part of the 19th century gives an impression of the range of activities in the town at that time.

One record book held by the Stornoway Trust as a successor to the Mackenzie and Matheson estates shows a whole range of jobs and conditions for people being granted feus between 1823 and 1825.

The occupations included shoemaker; Ground Officer; mason; the Steward of the sailing boat Prince Ernest Augustus; smith and joiner.

There were several widows, some with children. There were also wrights, shipbuilders, shipmasters and shipowners along with sailors and a Royal Navy sailing master.

Other occupations for those taking feus were cooper, cartwright, Customs clerk, shopkeeper, builder, wheelwright, carpenter and cabinet maker.

There was also a "writer in Edinburgh' a tailor, a house carpenter and a sawyer.

The largest numbers involved sea-related work. There were five shipowners, including one from Liverpool; four ship-masters; and three sailors. But there were five joiners, three smiths and three masons as well as four shoemakers. Certainly this gives a picture of a wide range of occupations in a flourishing community.

Artificial light ... the feu grant for the Stornoway Gas Light Company signed on September 27, 1849

The great years of the herring fishery

The great years of the herring fishery in the 19th and early 20th centuries saw Stornoway at its most cosmopolitan with thousands of extra workers living in the town during the height of the season. The peak of local activity was over the 20 years before the Great War of 1914-18, but from 1820 onwards the town was part of the general boom in Scottish herring fishing

One specialised area of work was that of The Herring Girls – Clann Nighean an Sgadain – who gutted and packed the fish at an average rate of one a second and there were tens of millions to process. Packing the fish in salt was the only way to preserve them for their long journey to their markets elsewhere in Britain, Germany and Russia. The Herring Girls not only worked in Stornoway during the fishing season but followed the harvest of the seas across Scotland and down the East Coast of England as well.

Outside interest in the fisheries is recorded from the visit of Sir Donald Monro to the Western Isles in 1549, when he compiled a description of the Islands which became part of a History of Scotland, by George Buchanan, published in 1582. He drew particular attention to the rich fishing near what is now the Braighe, saying that the two sea lochs, north and south of the church at Eye, were full of fish all the year round.

But early as 1550, James V of Scotland tried to organise a group of Fife fishermen to work from the Hebrides and this was repeated by James VI and Charles I in the next century as they tried to establish Lowland fishermen in Stornoway. The Royal attempts to take over the fishing were resisted by local people, aided by the Dutch fishermen who dominated the world of European herring until the 18th Century. The Dutch who operated from large decked boats or 'busses' with drift nets, barrels and salt and cured the herring aboard, fished mainly near the Scottish coasts. The Dutch may also have bought fish caught by local people. Certainly, Lord Seaforth, who bought Lewis in 1610, called on Dutch fishing expertise to exploit the rich waters of the Minch from Stornoway. That created controversy elsewhere in Scotland as competing burghs attempted to insist the Dutch be removed.

By the 1650s, Lewis and its fisheries were seen as such a lure to the Dutch that the Royalists offered Lewis to the Netherlands in return for Dutch support against the regime of Oliver Cromwell. In his book about the Hebrides, published in 1703, Skye man Martin Martin reported that the people of Stornoway had come to excel all their neighbours in the herring trade because of what they had learned from the Dutch about fishing and curing.

There was a major boost from the Union of Parliaments in 1707 which allowed Stornoway merchants access to markets in the British West Indies, North America and elsewhere. Stornoway continued to grow as a port throughout the 18th Century although the American War of Independence and the later loss of the American colonies cut off that market. The Salt Tax, introduced in 1712, provided an additional boost to Stornoway which until the end of the century was the only place on the West Coast north of Oban where salt, the essential preservative for fish, could be legally obtained. The tax was not abolished until 1825, although other salt warehouses and Customs houses had been built at Tobermory and Isle Martin near Ullapool by then. In 1763, Stornoway was the base for about 50 fishing boats. However, the main stimulus for expansion in Scotland overall came in the later years of that century when the Government was paying subsidies called bounties to encourage boatbuilding. A fleet of over 300 herring busses were eventually fitted out to catch herring mainly on the west coast. They were not very efficient, with the cost of the bounties often greater than the value of the herring cured. It was 1764 when a buss based in Stornoway sailed south for the first time to the agreed rendezvous point at Campbeltown. In 1785 the government introduced barrel bounties. This helped to increase actual production as opposed to the fitting out of boats. The barrel bounties were also available for open boats working along the coast. The curers who took the herring from the fishermen then started making engagements (contracts) with the fishermen before the season began so the fishermen were guaranteed a price for their herring.

In the last years of the 18th century the herring shoals ceased to come into the sea lochs of Lewis. Exports fell from almost 11,000 barrels in 1793 to less than 1,800 only three years later. Trade was also affected by the Napoleonic Wars, yet another example in the long history of the Western Isles herring industry where international affairs had a major impact.

Overall in Scotland, the increasing significance of the fisheries led in 1809 to the setting up of the Fishery Board. Fishery officers made sure herring were gutted before being packed and also inspected the barrels that were being used. The officers also compiled statistics of production. In the 1820s, despite protests, the bounties were ended. Nonetheless the fishery, particularly on the East Coast of Scotland, continued to expand.

The temporary shortage of herring in the seas around Lewis, combined with the collapse of the kelp industry after the end of the Napoleonic Wars, led to many Island fishermen moving seasonally to work from East Coast ports from Peterhead to Lerwick. In later years the women gutters and curers moved to join them and by the 1860s thousands were finding work on the mainland as the East Coast industry grew.

At first most of the cured herring was still going either to Ireland or the West Indian plantations, but sales fell after the freeing of the slaves in the 1830s and the Potato Famines of the 1840s in Ireland. However, as its quality became renowned, Scottish herring came to dominate the market in Europe after 1850. In the later 19th and early 20th century the Scottish herring fishery became the biggest fishery in the world. The development of much faster transport links by rail, plus the time saved by curing and packing on shore rather than at sea as the Dutch did, played a major role in this. Thus the speed and skill of the herring girls was crucial to the whole success of the industry.

Success meant East Coast fishermen, backed by the curers, invested in more and bigger boats and more nets but the expanded fishery was still largely confined to a summer season of about two months from mid-July when the migratory herring were off the coast in quantity. The East Coast vessels wanted a longer season which was most readily achieved by sailing to the west coast in the early summer. Here, herring were available in May and June. By the 1870s the fleet involved could exceed 1000 boats, and Stornoway's seasonal population would almost triple to around 9,000. In addition, new herring fishing stations were established on Lewis in places like Gress, Portnaguran, Bayble, Cromore and Holm.

In 1898, 700 fishing boats were using Stornoway in the summer season. By the end of the century large numbers of Scottish curers were also travelling to the English ports of Great Yarmouth and Lowestoft where, by 1900, the Scottish fleet outnumbered the big native fleet, as it did in Shetland where the herring season was also later in the year. In 1899, Stornoway fishermen sailed their own boats as far as Yarmouth for the first time. The zenith of the herring fishery was between 1900 and World War I when the steam drifter became the main means of catching herring. Almost all the locally owned boats now had decking, rather than being open like the traditional sgoth, and some used steam hauling gear to deal with their sails and nets.

Originally, families had worked together as economic units with the women gutting the herring which the men caught and baiting the lines they used to catch white fish in the winter. Children might also be involved in collecting the bait for the hooks. However, as the herring industry developed, the work became more specialised and curing firms took on the task of organising the processing labour force. Family links remained important because the female workforce would often be related to, or married to, the fishermen or to the coopers and others involved in the industry. The women were employed in the curing yards as gutters and packers, working in teams or crews of three – two to gut and one to pack. The curer employed one team for every boat he engaged. The packer was in charge of the team and dealt with the curer. The herring girls began their nomadic work when they were around 16 years old – and sometimes continued into their sixties.

Gutting work was hard, and the women were expected to work long hours. They worked six-day weeks, but never on a Sunday, when they attended church. There were also a variety of organisations – such as the Red Cross, the Church of Scotland, and the Mission to Fisherfolk – who looked after their physical and social welfare.

In the Victorian era, if the catch was good, the women might start at 5am or whenever the catch first became available and work for 12 to 15 hours or even longer. Because they were paid on a piecework basis, and because the fish could not be kept for too long unprocessed, they had to work non-stop until all the catch was gutted and packed. They would eat a 'piece' and drink a mug of tea as they worked. From 1913 onwards, the hours began to be regulated. At first, this was based on a 10 and 13 hour alternating shift pattern. The women often sang while they waited for the fish and if there was any spare time, they would get out their knitting (they knitted clothes, particularly Guernsey woollens, for the fishermen and others). The teams usually worked outside in all weathers. They wore oilskin overalls to protect their clothes. Later on they also wore heavy duty Wellington boots. The gutters wrapped their fingers in strips of cloth – cloots – to protect them from the sharp knives and the brine. The cloths also helped them to hold the slippery fish. On average, at the height of the season's work, one girl could gut a herring every second so a crew of three filled 30 barrels a day on average. One crew in 1924 packed 37 barrels in one day, a total which gives some impression of the numbers of fish caught at the time as that would mean three women dealt with about 37,000 fish on their own in a single shift.

Even in 1938, there was a total of 1000 women engaged in gutting, packing and kippering in Stornoway, most of whom went on to work in East Anglia later in the year. It was estimated that they earned £16 at the local summer fishing and £15 in East Anglia. In 1939, six herring girls from Lewis were flown back from the Orkney fishing season by the pioneering Highland aviator Captain E. E.Fresson. The six seater De Havilland Dragon plane was owned by Scottish Airways and made the journey in less than an hour, cutting out a ferry and train journey that would have taken several days. The grass runway at Stornoway had just opened for commercial flights but these ended soon afterwards because of the start of World War Two.

There were a whole range of other occupations which depended on the existence of the herring industry. For instance, the boxes that held the kippers were put together in their thousands by schoolboys working after school for pocket money. The wood came in flat-packs ready to be nailed together – box-makers could be recognised by their blackened fingernails, injured by mishits with the hammers! For the white herring, the coopers – barrel-makers – were an essential part of the industry. Millions of barrels were produced but few, if any, survive as they were sent abroad or burned for firewood. Then there were the carters for transport, the shipwrights and repairers. Ships were regularly built in Stornoway until the start of the 20th century and the end of the era of sail.

The First World War dealt a massive blow to the Hebridean herring fishery. The islands lost thousands of men who were killed or severely injured in the fighting and in the sinking of the Iolaire on New Year's Day 1919. Many fishing boats became unusable as they lay abandoned during the war. In addition, there were no longer sales to the former overseas markets in Russia which had become the USSR following the triumph of the Communists, and in economically-stricken post-war Germany. The fishery continued on a smaller scale and had to suffer illegal trawling by boats from Aberdeen, Fleetwood and other big mainland ports.

Because of the capital investment needed, the vast majority of the steam drifters involved in the herring fishery were from off the Island. In 1938 there were 111 steam-boats involved at Stornoway, of which only five were locally registered. There were also motorboats and two sailing boats involved. The East Coast boats were twice the size on average of the local boats which only took about one fifth of the total tonnage caught.

During World War Two fishing continued from Stornoway with boats coming from as far as Fife for up to 16 weeks at a time. After the war the tradition of the Herring Girls died away as the processing was mechanised. Nationally, eating habits changed and herring was no longer sought after. Commercially, Stornoway found itself unable to compete with mainland ports, particularly Mallaig. As the numbers of herring being caught fell, systems for catching them were improved from the use of drifters, to ringnetters, to trawlers and finally, in the 1960s, the purse seine or purse net. Designed originally in Norway, the use of these nets, combined with sonar detection of shoals, left the herring with little chance of escape. In the 1970s the fishery was closed.

Number 3 Pier on South Beach in around 1920

Lazy Corner on the town's North Beach and Cromwell Street quays is pictured at the height of the work of the herring industry.
Perceval Square is in the background

A clear view of South Beach as it looked in the late 1950s with the Maritime Buildings and the Fish Mart on No 1 Pier and the original Caledonian Hotel towering over the houses on Churchyard Lane

This painting by John Clayton Adams is dated 1867 … it is a puzzle that the Castle conservatory is shown, left, as that was not completed until 1875

This image from the early 20th century shows the castle and Cuddy Point clearly, with the Lewis Combination Poorhouse glowering in the distance. The Bayhead River is still its original form, winding into the distance along the side of the road, showing that the main depth of the river was actually the other side of the valley from its present channel

A view of Stornoway quayside during the late 1930s showing the art deco harbour building on No 1 pier with the old Fish Mart beside it Further along Carn House stands next to the rebuilt Town Hall where Carn Gardens are now; the Louise Carnegie Hostel fills the space where An Lanntair Arts centre now stands, and the Playhouse Cinema dominates the corner opposite. At the end of James Street stands an 18th century house which was similar to the one still standing next to Carn Gardens. It was among those demolished in 1962 to create the Ross and Cromarty Council building now occupied by the Western Isles NHS Board. Newalls mill fills the space to right of No 3 pier where the supermarket car park now is. Visible in the background to the left are new houses going up along Nicolson Road and in the distance, the Lewis Hospital and the Lewis Combination Poor House. Beyond the Clock Tower of The Nicolson Institute to the right, green fields reach out towards Sandwick. Also visible to the right are the brick-built Old Co-op Yard Buildings, built around 1900, originally a sawmill and builders merchant's yard and converted to become the head office of the former Western Isles Enterprise in 1999.

IN THE GLEN STORNOWAY.

What later became known as the "Sanny" bridge in Willowglen seen in earlier times. The County Sanatorium, later Hospital, was built after the First World War across the Lochs Road opposite the entrance to this part of the Castle Grounds. The hospital treated diseases like TB which were then a major threat to health. It was replaced in 1993 by the Western Isles Hospital. Its site is now an enterprise park.

Stornoway's architectural ironwork – preserved unlike so much similar work elsewhere because it was not melted down in World War Two – has now been recognised as of national significance after a study by Historic Scotland and several major exhibitions. In many cases Stornoway provides the only surviving evidence of the work of foundries from throughout Scotland. As important but less visible, Stornoway also pioneered the use of concrete in domestic buildings,

Above, Sir James Matheson's steam yacht turned mainland ferry link, the Mary Jane. Built in 1846 in Glasgow, she was used in the Minch until 1851. She is pictured here in later years after being converted into the Glencoe.
© Scottish Maritime Museum Licensor www.scran.co.uk

Left, The Ondine, bought by Sir James Matheson in 1871 to provide a service to the mainland. She was originally built in Blackwall, London, 1847 for the Royal Mail service between Dover and Calais.
© Glasgow City Council Licensor www.scran.co.uk

Working on a ship in the Patent Slip shipyard

A 19th century French etching entitled Stornoway boats return from the herring fishing

Stornoway takes to the high seas

In 1850, the tea clipper *Stornoway*, pictured left, was launched at the Aberdeen shipyard of Alexander Hall. She was one of the first of a series of revolutionary designs produced by that shipyard in the early 1850s; a super-fast sailing ship with a streamlined hull designed to carry the tea harvest back from China. The *Stornoway* marked a particular stage in the evolution of this design, which derived from Alexander Hall's unique "Aberdeen bow" designed for earlier schooners and clippers. Owned by Jardine Matheson, the Hong Kong-based trading firm, the clipper was named *Stornoway* because the firm's co-founder Sir James Matheson had just bought the Isle of Lewis.

In the 1850s, the British national newspapers never tired of repeating the names of the *Stornoway* and other clippers from the same shipyard such as *Chrysolite* and *Cairngorm*. The Stornoway was built as British shipyards were producing new clippers at a great rate. This allowed their owners to compete with large, fast American ships, permitted for the first time to ship cargoes into British ports following the repeal of the Navigation Acts in 1849. They

were also designed to serve the new trade routes to South Africa and Australia, boosted by the Australian Gold Rush of the 1850s. (The Gold Rush left ships denuded of their crews in Sydney Harbour as sailors sometimes simply jumped overboard and swam ashore to get a chance to make their fortunes - the ships' captains had to offer additional pay rises to keep their crews intact.)

Stornoway was a 595 ton vessel – in 1852, the vast new American clipper *Nightingale*, weighing in at 1060 tons, reported meeting the British ships *Stornoway*, *Chrysolite* and *Challenger* along the China Coast. The renowned *Cutty Sark*, launched in 1869 at Dumbarton, was 963 tons. However, *Stornoway* was one of eight clippers built in Aberdeen between 1848 and 1856 which exerted considerable influence on the developing theories of fast sailing on both sides of the Atlantic. At the time Aberdeen was seen as so pre-eminent in such designs that journalists' reports tended to assume such vessels were built there even if they had actually been built in Liverpool or Glasgow to the same style.

Stornoway made 12 voyages between the Far East and Britain between 1851 and 1867 – but the fastest transit was 104 days from the Pearl River, north of Hongkong, to London. The record was 85 days, set by *Scawfell* in 1861. *Stornoway's* last tea voyage was in 1867 between Hong Kong and London when she took 114 days. After that, she moved to other trades. In June 1873, she was wrecked on the Kentish Knock sandbank in the Thames estuary.

The direct involvement of Stornoway folk in the development of the clipper is shown by the way that John Robertson, the son of a collector of customs in Stornoway, was, as the commander of the *Stornoway*, instrumental in bringing to the attention of Jardine Matheson the building of the new *Cairngorm* clipper at Alexander Hall's in 1853. By this time the shipyard was building new designs of clipper on a speculative basis, depending on its reputation to get sales. The recommendation from John Robertson, who had commanded many clippers, was sufficient for Jardine Matheson to decide to add *Cairngorm* to their fleet.

The picture above displays the the interior of the former conservatory outside Lews Castle in full bloom. The conservatory survived until after World War Two, enabled a very wide variety of exotic plants, shrubs and trees from all over the world to survive on Lewis. A few even survived out in the open for some years after the structure was dismantled. The work to create the Lews Castle Grounds began soon after the Matheson purchase of Lewis in 1844. Initially the gardens involved only a small area of land around the former Seaforth Lodge which stood where the Castle is today. But this was extended to cover 600 acres of formal and informal gardens with specimens of trees and shrubs from all around the world. The conservatory was added in 1875, just before the death of Sir James Matheson.

Major Duncan Matheson, the last of the Mathesons to own the Castle, can be seen, left, in the foreground of the picture at a time when the formal gardens were in their full glory.

The original building of The Nicolson Institute was opened on Thursday 27 February 1873, in the presence of its Trustees, local dignitaries and parents, when the keys were handed over to the newly appointed Headmaster, Mr John Sutherland, formerly Head Teacher of the General Assembly School in the town which joined this new establishment with all 105 of its pupils. In January 1893, the then headmaster, Mr John Forbes, was placed in charge of the new Secondary department which introduced the teaching of Latin, Greek, Mathematics, Geography, History, English, French, German, Music, Domestic Economy, Drawing and Needlework. Today, there is no trace of this first building of the Nicolson Institute. The clock tower, which still remains, was an addition in 1902, with a clock and chimes added in 1905. The Clock School, as it became known, was demolished in 1972 to make way for the Nicolson-Lewis Sports Centre, itself now demolished.

The Matheson era in Stornoway industry

Stornoway Harbour is dominated by Lews Castle, built by Sir James Matheson and his wife Mary Jane after they paid £190,000 for the Isle of Lewis in 1844, and it remains an enduring symbol of their influence and wealth. It was, however, a symbol of oppression for those were involved in 19th and early 20th century disputes in the crofting communities.

The Matheson era saw a whole range of industrial and social developments for Stornoway, plus the transformation of the land on the other side of the harbour into the Lews Castle Grounds which we know today. The modern historical perspective on the Mathesons and on their successor Lord Leverhulme who owned Lewis from 1918-23 has been dominated by their conflicts with the crofting communities. However, the situation for Stornoway was different – when the Mathesons came into conflict with the merchants and shipowners over harbour developments, for instance, they generally failed to impose their opinions.

Stornoway has accommodated many industries over the centuries, belying the image of the Hebrides as a purely agricultural region. For instance, the Newton/Inaclete area has hosted many ventures, from shipbuilding, kippering and fish processing through to Harris Tweed production and, in modern times, television production and freight transport.

Sir James was instrumental in establishing a range of industries – from the gasworks (on part of the site now used by the Tesco supermarket) to the brickworks at Garrabost in Point. He spent more than £30,000 on a project to create oil from peat, which involved pioneering research and engineering work of international importance.

He also backed the building of the Patent Slip which cost £6000 and provided a major boost to the local shipbuilding industry. In 1838, there were 11 shipbuilders in Stornoway; by 1885 this had risen to 13; but by 1898 there was only one; and none were left by 1931. The Patent Slip was the largest shipyard and it took up much of the land that Tesco and its car park now occupies. For many years after the closure of the yard, this area used by the former Newalls Tweed Mill of which only the front offices now survive along lower James Street.

Above, Sir James and Lady Matheson; below a shooting party outside the Castle

The yard had a huge chimney for a massive steam engine that worked the Slip by hauling ships up for repair. The Patent Slip was constructed in the early years of Sir James Matheson's ownership of Lewis and created a boom in ship construction, and in ancillary trades. It was termed a Patent Slip because it was an original design which gave the town a commercial advantage but sadly its years of high production were limited as the wooden vessels which were its mainstay were displaced by iron ships built elsewhere.

Rev R. M. Stephen (1861-1916) in his recollections of Stornoway called *Glimpses of Portrona*, recalled schoolboy memories of the Slip as youngsters slipped away from classes to watch the launching of new ships and of other ships which had been repaired. New builds were increasingly rare in his time – because of the change from wood to iron for hulls of ships. He says the slip's heyday was before his childhood but writing around 1910 he warns those who had not seen it since their young days:"The place will sadden them. The bones of the Slip are still there; there is even some flesh left on them; but the soul is fled." It was now nothing like his schooldays. What charm was there in schoolwork, he says, when you could be seeing "the great engine working and the great wheels go round, or joining the carpenters as they drew the cradle up by hand to the accompanying shanty: – Rio! Rio! Rio! Rio!, I'm off to the Rio Grand…

"We watched with unflagging interest the growth of a ship – a dear old wooden ship – from the laying of the keel when, with colours flying and men lustily cheering, she slid down the "ways" into the sea."

He tells of a schooner which lingered in the yard throughout much of his boyhood before it finally found an owner and was launched – removing what had become a town landmark. "A rare spectacle like the launching of a new ship brought the whole town flocking to the Slip: but even common launches in the repairing Slip sufficed to attract a crowd of boys."

In 1857 it was proposed to have a canal cut from Stornoway to Broadbay. Until the expansion of the industrial estates in Newton in the 20th century, there was a narrow drainage channel which ran right across the peninsula from Broadbay to the harbour. It now ends at Sandwick Road. The proposed canal was of a different scale, with locks and bridges. It would have carried barges carting clay and coals from Garrabost. Engineering levels were taken and tenders invited for the project which it was estimated would cost £900. However, work never seems to have started.

Among the industries formerly established in the Stornoway area were kelp production and whisky distilling – the distillery was in the Shoe Burn valley just beside the inner harbour from around 1830 to 1857. There was also oil refining – both from peat and from fish oil – as well as brickmaking, kippering, fishcanning and, much later, oilrig construction.

Inaclete/Newton was a mass of kippering sheds by the end of the 19th century with what is now called Inaclete Road being called Kipper Road. An issue of the Stornoway Historical Society Journal in the year 2000 carried a recollection of boyhood visits to the area: "There, in vast caverns, we watched the kipperers disappear in the smoke to build row upon row, tier upon tier of split herrings – later to retrieve them as kippers. There, in yards full of staves and hoops, we watched fag-smoking coopers bending fire and iron, wood and water to their will, shaping beautiful symmetrical barrels. There, too, in the upper regions, we watched the apprentices take three square shapes of wood and three long ones and make a kipper box."

Around Lews Castle, the gardens, the forested hills and valleys, the roadways and pathways, along with a complex but largely hidden drainage system, were all created by the Mathesons. Sir James commissioned the renowned architect Charles Wilson to design the castle. Seaforth Lodge, which stood on the same site, was largely demolished to make way for the new building. Building work started in 1847 and the £60,000 project took seven years to complete. A further £49,000 was spent on transforming the rough grazing land around the new Castle into extensive woodlands and private gardens. The temperate climate and shelter from the initial planting of hardy species, created ideal growing conditions for a wide range of native and imported species.

The new castle was further extended with a tennis court and the conservatory on the south side added in 1875 by Alex Sutherland. This housed a host of more exotic and delicate species which survived until 1950 when it was demolished. Some of the exotic plants survived out in the open for a few more years.

On September 2, 1902, the Castle was visited by King Edward VII and Queen Alexandra and two silver firs planted by the royal couple survive today near the site of the former conservatory.

Sir James Matheson died in 1878 after a childless marriage and his wife ran the estate until her death in 1896, when it passed to her husband's nephew Donald, who passed it on to his son Lieutenant-Colonel Duncan Matheson after he died in 1901. Lieutenant-Colonel Matheson sold it to the Bolton-born soap magnate Lord Leverhulme in 1918 and Lord Leverhulme ran the Island until 1923.

In the aftermath of his tenure, the people of Stornoway Parish – covering the Broadbay area – accepted his offer of the land and the Stornoway Trust was formed, as a democratically elected community landowner.

Work to restore the Matheson Monument in the Castle Grounds was one of two major renewal schemes involving investment totalling more than £300,000 in 2005-6. Backed by a range of public, community and private groups, the projects involved the reconstruction of a waterwheel to provide a visitor facility and to generate electricity as well as the restoration of the Lady Matheson monument and garden. The waterwheel originally powered a flour mill built in 1816 and burned down in 1890.

The garden and monument was built in 1880 by Lady Matheson, in memory of her husband. The Lady Matheson Memorial Garden project aimed to re-establish the view of the marble monument and the outlook from it across the harbour, and to repair the monument. Railings surrounding the site were restored and extra paths built. Until work started on the restoration scheme, the memorial was largely hidden and inaccessible. The surrounding garden was once a lovely area, but had become neglected so the plan included repairing stone walls, steps and balustrade. The area was restored with money from Forward Scotland, Western Isles Enterprise, the Stornoway Amenity Trust, Historic Scotland, and the Stornoway Trust.

Major Duncan Matheson on one of the sets of stepping stones which linked Bayhead and the Castle Grounds. The locations are shown in the map. Before the Grounds were created, the stones formed the start of the route to the former village of Ranol and to Lochs.

Peat experiments prove bad for fish

In the year 1860, the hopes for industrial development on the Isle of Lewis were at their highest. The herring fishery was providing seasonal work for thousands of men and women both on and off the Island; and various schemes started by landowner Sir James Matheson were generating work for hundreds more. There was road and bridge construction, shipbuilding was booming in Stornoway, the gasworks was operating as well as the brickworks at Garrabost, and there were several educational establishments for both boys and girls that put the town ahead of its region in an era before universal education had been started by the Government.

The most revolutionary of all the projects was the Lewis Chemical Works at Marybank and the associated Garrabost Oil Refinery, which attracted the attention of some of the most eminent scientists of that era, some of whom came to Lewis to see them. These two plants made up the most advanced peat-to-oil distillation process in the world. Work on this project began in the mid 1850s. This was before the full-scale exploitation of underground oil resources across the world. At that time a desperate search was being undertaken for sources of oil to replace those which came largely from animals and plants.

October 1860 saw the most spectacular demonstration of the power of the materials being used at the Lewis Chemical Works – and how little was known about how to handle them. On the day of the disaster, the resident scientist, Dr Benjamin Paul, had given instructions for the ten kilns to be kindled in a particular sequence after an eight-day stoppage of production to try to remedy some of the earlier problems. An hour after Dr Paul left the works, with only six of the furnaces so far lit, there was a massive explosion as the gases involved were ignited by a spark.

According to Donald Morison, who had constructed the works at Marybank, the blast smashed "several of the cast-metal tanks to pieces, scattering the galvanised pipes and crossends in all directions, shaking the earth, and causing the dishes in the nearest house (460 yards distant) to rattle on the table. In Stornoway it was thought to (be)

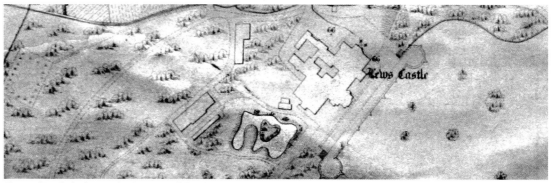

Lews Castle in its early days … with a large lake including an artificial island where the tennis courts and the conservatory were later established

thunder." It was, Mr Morison says, "nothing less than a miracle" that the men on duty survived. Work, however, was scarcely interrupted. A squad of men were called in to repair the works and wooden tanks substituted for the cast iron ones. Eight days later, the works were ready to be kindled again.

However, the noxious gases continued to pose dangers for the workers trying to put peat in the kilns. Mr Morison describes how there was a "fresh relay of men in the open air ready to haul out any that would succumb" and bring them round with "buckets of water on his face and head." On one occasion, three men were hauled out and left stretched out in a delirious state for several hours. They were off work for two days with the after-effects. In addition, people living in both town and country were complaining of "the sickening and offensive smell from the works."

Carbonic Oxide gas had been pouring out of the kilns when they were being refilled with peat, making the workers feel sick, and spreading a smell for miles downwind of the works. The chimney at the works had been spewing out peat tar (which was supposed to be kept inside the equipment to be refined!) and during snow, the brown stain stretched half-a-mile down wind of the works.

There had been earlier problems – during an experimental period in 1857-9 under the supervision of Mr Henry Caunter, the fish in an ornamental lake near to Lews Castle had been killed by pollution, and the fish in the Creed river continued to be affected by the full-scale plant at Marybank after 1859.

The first experimental chemical works built on Marybank by Mr Caunter were about 30 yards from the works later designed by Dr Paul and seem to have been beside a small stream which crosses under the Tarbert road before the Creed Bridge. These works were supplied by peat brought by a boat on a canal of three-quarters of a mile length, the course of which can still be seen winding across the moor.

The crisis following the explosion led to a confrontation between Mr Morison as foreman and Dr Paul and also with the notorious factor to the Matheson estate, Donald Munro. Mr Morison shows that the basic problem was a lack of scientific knowledge anywhere else for them to draw on in constructing the plant. A similar project in Ireland had collapsed because it had failed to overcome the practical problems involved. Dr Paul and Mr Caunter went to Germany to see a peat-oil works there and were astonished to find it in a very primitive state, using herring barrels from Stornoway as condensers, all connected with leaky wooden pipes. Mr Morison says: "The absence of a similar work anywhere made it impossible to get a man with practical knowledge to act as foreman under Dr Paul." Referring to himself, Mr Morison comments: "In this case Dr Paul and his foreman were similar, learning through disappointments and failures."

After the explosion, Mr Morison had to contend with an angry Dr Paul – he "firmly told" him that all his orders had been followed about lighting the kilns. Then Donald Munro appeared and "expressed hope that we would attend to Messrs Paul and Caunter's directions in future and not explode and smash the works again."

Mr Morison comments that this "only shows how gentlemen make scapegoats of those under them." Donald Munro's training as a lawyer showed through, however. Mr Morison says that because of his "knowledge of cross-questioning, he left the works with…the knowledge that orders for kindling were strictly adhered to." Finally, in the spring of 1861, Dr Paul went south to England to get more advice and technical support about how to proceed with the work. This led to a full-scale reconstruction of the plant and production was restarted.

The works, constructed under Mr Morison's supervision in 1859 and over later years, included ten tar kilns side by side which were cylindrical brick chambers 5ft in diameter and 12ft high, with a fire-grate of about 2ft area at the lower end, and a hopper, with a lid on the top, for introducing the peat. From the side of each kiln passed pipe about 1ft in diameter which connected to main pipe that was 3ft in diameter and extended all round the range of kilns and from which the tar vapour from the kilns was discharged. The vapour was passed through a series of pipes and flues and thence into a large flue running about 50 yards up the side of a hill, on top of which was placed a chimney 30ft high. The product collected in the condensers and the tar was separated from water and other byproducts by heating it in a large boiler and skimming it off the surface.

A tramroad ran along the top of the kilns, communicating with the tramroads diverging across the moor, for bringing up the supplies of peat. There were almost four miles of tramways on the moor. At the works there was an 8-inch steam engine – a stationary installation

This is Caunter's Corner, named after Mr Henry Caunter who moved to Stornoway from Devon with James Matheson. He played a key role in development and orginsiation of the Lewis Chemical Works and related projects. He also was one of the early amateur enthusiasts for research into fossils and was called in by the Stornoway Pier and Harbour Commission to draw up plans for an extension of the harbour wall between William Morrison's quay and the Lewis Hotel Quay in 1876. In 1857 he proposed a ship canal linking Stornoway Harbour and Broadbay as he was going to expand the clay diggings at Garrabost and dig for coal there, too, it was reported at the time. He and his younger daughter lived in the cottage on the corner, then called Millburn Cottage, and now Glen House. The photograph was probably taken at the end of a Market Day. The Caberfeidh Hotel grounds now occupy the land on the right, formerly Manor Farm.

– which was used to draw the peat trucks up the incline to the kilns, and later to power a fan which was installed to improve air-flow through the kilns.

After the explosion and various other setbacks, the works was reconstructed to prevent the build up of explosive gases. The work included elevating the condensers five feet above the ground, placed in double rows each side of the gangway that supported the tramway. The kiln furnaces were fitted with ashpits and fire doors, as well as apparatus to prevent deadly gases escaping. There were four tall scrubbers adjoining the fan which had water pumped through them by the engine to extract the final residues of tar before the gases reached the fan. Water joints were added to the condensers, similar to those used in gasworks like the one in Stornoway itself. The main chimney was now connected to the boiler furnace, rather than the condensers and kilns, reducing the problem with back draughts and the dangerous mixing of air, fire and explosive gasses. Strangely, despite the fact of the explosion, more time passed before it was realised that the gases which were still causing sickness for the staff and smells in the wider environment could be simply burned off and a mechanism was constructed to do this.

Mr Morison describes the complex at Garrabost in some detail. The refinery apparatus was built in the extensive brickworks sheds, with a large steam boiler and pan shed. Dr Paul had a cottage built for himself where in 1861 he was living with two male servants.

The total staff in Garrabost, as listed by Mr Morison at the time of Dr Paul's return to England in 1862, was at least ten, with an additional squad of labourers. The staff included blacksmiths, carpenters, a clerk, an engine fitter and riveter and the brickmakers as well.

It seems the brickworks was chosen for the location simply because it was there already – there is no explanation given for the initial decision to divide the refinery from the Lewis Chemical Works. This led to a further separation of sites when it became clear there was not enough water available at the brickworks site. A distilling works was built lower down the valley from where the Garrabost Mill now stands. A half-mile of tramway, the cuttings and trackbeds of which can still be seen, was built to connect the brickworks with the new site. This seems to have involved a complex of trackbeds and junctions at the New Garrabost end of the moor where existing tramways led out across the moor.

Mr Morison calls the decision to disperse the works over three sites, separated by up to six miles " an enormous reckless blunder" and comments that Mr Caunter and Dr Paul, as the "responsible parties" used the "more refined term" of "an error of judgement." Mr Morison says that because of difficulty with getting the distillate back up the hill to the brickworks site, operating entirely by using manpower to push the trucks up the 1 in 30 incline, the costs of transporting it over that half-mile were equal to those of moving the tar from Marybank to Garrabost, all of which would have been unnecessary if the works had been placed on one site. This created an "enormous expense" for Sir James Matheson.

In 1865, Mr Caunter seems to have realised something

Dr Benjamin H Paul sketched in 1893 when he was an expert witness in a court case

had to be done about this problem and got Sir James Matheson's permission to build a new peat distillation plant like the Creed Works only half-a-mile from the refinery on Point. Mr Morison supervised this work – but after £1600 had been spent the works were still only slightly more than half finished although Mr Caunter's estimate to Sir James had been for a total cost of only £1400. The new works were abandoned, left for several years and then demolished. The engine and the boiler were transferred to the sawmill at the Patent Slip. The project was finally shut down in 1874.

Dr Paul seems to have been a larger-than-life character. An article of reminiscences published in the Oban Times in 1887 written by a Stornowegian then living in Campbeltown, recalled how Dr Paul was regarded as "cracked" by his neighbours on Point. He had a "Norwegian charger" on which he took riding exercises and was prone to "keeping the folk in terror" by riding pellmell between Garrabost and the canal at the edge of Stornoway. Dr Paul was also a close friend of several of those involved in the pre-Raphaelite Brotherhood of artists and writers and had been a student of pharmacy from the age of 14,

including studies at the world-beating German university of Giessen where he got his doctorate at the age of 20. He was one of the first eight students at England's School of Pharmacy.

It is not known why Dr Paul suddenly abandoned the Chemical Works in 1862. He had clearly not fallen out with the project because he went on to give major speeches about it to the Society of Arts and to the British Association – the topmost contemporary forums for discussion of scientific progress. Furthermore, he returned to the island at least once (in 1865) to see how the project was working and may have been instrumental in supporting the stream of renowned scientists who visited Lewis. He remained in contact with foreman Mr Morison for some, if not many, years. Mr Morison told the story of the departure in his memoir written in 1895 which outlined the whole saga. In the first week of April 1862, Dr Paul, "looked unusually out of sorts," writes Mr Morison. He "remarked it likely that he was soon to leave the Works." Mr Morison states that Dr Paul frankly told him the reasons for such a sudden change. And then tantalisingly adds: "Not necessary here to repeat." Dr Paul left for London on "the first steamer" and it was not known for ten days whether he would stay away. But then it was confirmed he would never return to his work.

Dr Paul was aged 30 when he arrived on Lewis. In the 1861 census, he described himself as a gentleman living in Garrabost. He was clearly an impressive character and a demon of energy like so many of the great characters of the Victorian Age. He had created a major research establishment in Garrabost – including an English analytical chemist, William Whitehead, who moved there with his wife Elizabeth and their son who was aged one in 1861. A fully equipped chemistry laboratory was among the facilities. There were several other staff and a lot of additional buildings.

Back in London, Dr Paul spent the late 1860s working hard to get his career back on track in experimental chemistry – before becoming the editor of the Pharmaceutical Society journal between 1870 and 1902. He died in February 1917 and subsequent obituaries and letters in professional journals make clear that everyone knew him as someone truly unwilling to suffer fools gladly.

Memories of Donald Munro

Donald Munro was probably the most notorious character in the history of 19th century Stornoway. His extraordinary combination of administrative and legal powers is detailed in the book *A Shilling For Your Scowl*, by James Shaw Grant, whose own family was one of the victims of Munro's legal vendettas.

At the summit of his career, he held nearly 30 public offices. He was both Procurator Fiscal and Factor of Lewis and he was also Captain of the Militia. This meant he headed the only military force permanently on the island and often threatened to use it. He was one of only two solicitors practising on Lewis – and the other was his cousin, William Ross, who was his business partner. He was chairman of four Parochial Boards and legal adviser to the those boards as well. He also chaired four island school boards, and was also vice chairman of the harbour trustees, chief magistrate of Stornoway, deputy chairman of the road trust and a director of both gas and water companies.

This meant he could appear in the local Sheriff Court as both prosecutor and solicitor, and also sat on the bench as a Justice of the Peace, while he also held the ancient title of Baron Bailie and had to right to convene his own courts. He was also a commissioner for supply and a commissioner under the Income Tax Acts.

Incidentally, Mr Ross held a series of other legal positions – for instance, he was secretary and treasurer to the Harbour Trust. Other Munro relatives were involved as well. For instance, John Rose, a nephew of Munro, was a ground officer for the Stornoway Parish with extensive knowledge of crofting affairs.

James Shaw Grant remarks that only Munro's role as captain of the Matheson Cricket Team was one which did not allow a further chance to oppress the general population – although one must have the suspicion that opponents might have found it convenient to lose to Munro's team! It is notable, for instance, that in July 1857, at the competition organised by the Stornoway Horticultural Society, it was Munro who took many of the first prizes – including first for the Best Six Cut Roses, first for the Best Six Pansies, first for the Best Three Early Cabbages and First for the Best Early

Carrots. The garden at Lews Castle was established as soon as the building work was over and by 1856 was growing all manner of decorative plants as well as pears, peaches, nectarines, plums, cherries, grapes and other fruit in a variety of glasshouses. However, the head gardener at Lews Castle in 1857, a Mr Conlon, was also the judge for the Horticultural Society and may well have had personal reasons for feeling that Munro, Factor of the Estate for four years by then, was the appropriate recipient of top prizes.

Munro, who was both a Highlander and a Gaelic speaker, clearly had a fearsome temper. Roderick Campbell from Ness, author of a memoir called *The Father of St Kilda*, published in 1901, recalls his own confrontation with Munro as a fourteen-year-old. He was working as what was termed a "herd loon", looking after cattle for the Estate. "I spent my days alone in a large walled park of about forty acres, having as sole companions a dozen or more Irish cows. I had plenty of time to spare for deep meditations, the first and foremost subject being my future prospects."

He had missed a lot of schooling because of the impact of The Disruption on parochial schools in his area but he began to regret this lack of education as he saw other boys going past on the way to school in Stornoway. "At last out of my daily meditations grew the audacious resolution to ask the bailiff to allow me to go to school two hours in the forenoon and two hours in the afternoon. In return I was willing to sacrifice all my wages.

"I was prepared to point out to the bailiff that, as the park was walled, my being there made no difference whatsoever to the cows; they would eat and digest just as much grass in my absence as in my presence.

"I went to Sandey Buey, the bailiff. He received my plea with a smile, which showed me that my proposition was to be left indefinitely unconsidered. A higher authority, however, was over the understeward, the inexorable estate factor himself. And with bated breath and beating heart, and limbs quivering like an aspen leaf, to him I went. A perilous business I felt it to be to face a man so powerful and in religious matters, as I had been taught, so "unsound."

"On being ushered into the august presence of the titular governor of the Long Island, I felt as if seized by a sudden attack of lockjaw." He could barely bring himself to speak at all.

"Munro sharply asked my business. Drawing my slender frame up to its full height, I boldly repeated the logical proposition concerning the cows and the grass which the bailiff had treated with such scant respect. His face, anything but amiable in his better moods, gathered itself into a grimness altogether terrifying.

"You impudent fellow, your audacity surpasses anything in my experience. Do you think I am going to feed and pay you to go to school? You could learn nothing if you did go to school. Fishing and planting a few potatoes need no schooling. Nonsense! Impudence! Away with you instantly!"

Interestingly, in a fierce exchange of views in the columns of The Scotsman newspaper after Munro lost his job as Factor almost 20 years later, a Stornoway man was quoted as saying: "Mr Munro took no interest whatsoever in the education of the people – his great aim was to keep them in thorough ignorance. It was very different with his predecessor – for Mr Munro Mackenzie, during his reign, took the greatest possible interest in all our schools, and had them regularly examined in his own presence." (In contrast, Munro's partner William Ross, who became secretary to all the Lewis school boards, was remembered after his death in 1896 as the man who "built" the schools of Lewis.)

However, Roderick Campbell did not give up his personal quest for education. He defied Munro and stayed to argue. "I pled long and earnestly, asking at last but one hour daily. But my remonstrances might as well have been addressed to the stones of the street for all the impression they made upon him.

"Finally he got so angry that he told me he would send me to prison instead of to school if I did not leave his office sharp, for he didn't want an idiot in his service. The threat of prison was more alarming to me than even the monotonous prospect of watching the cows eat grass, so, choosing the least of two evils, I then and there threw down the seals of office with the title and emoluments, of "herd loon" upon the floor and speedily found myself in the street."

This confrontation ultimately led Roderick Campbell to leave for Canada and work successfully with the Hudson Bay Company for many years.

Contact with Munro also drove another Lewisman to emigrate to Canada and become even more of a success story. This was Robertson Macaulay, born ten years earlier than Roderick Campbell, but who also met Munro when he was in his early teens. His father was Kenneth Macaulay, a fishing boat skipper, who was born in Uig, but settled in Fraserburgh where he married Margaret Noble, and where Robertson was born in 1833. Robertson came to Stornoway at the age of ten to live with his aunt and emigrated to Canada in 1854. In 1856, he started working at the Canada Life Assurance Company as an accountant where he would remain until 1872. He then worked for the Mutual Life Association of Canada until becoming secretary of the Sun Mutual Life Insurance Company of Montreal (later the Sun Life Assurance Company of Canada) in 1874. Sun Mutual had been incorporated in 1865 but unfavourable economic conditions delayed plans and it only started business in 1871. In 1884, he was appointed managing director and was named president in 1889 succeeding the first president, Thomas Workman.

Robertson Macaulay retired as managing director in 1908 and was succeeded by his son, Thomas Bassett Macaulay, who later assisted the rebuilding of the Stornoway Town Hall as well as backing pioneering agricultural developments in both Canada and Scotland. He also set up the Macaulay Educational Trust for Lewis. Robertson died in 1915.

The *Canadian Dictionary of National Biography* (CDNB) outlines the impact that Donald Munro's behaviour had on the young Robertson's ideas of personal integrity and social responsibility. Munro only moved to Lewis from Tain in 1841 but was immediately involved in estate matters, particularly evictions. The CDNB entry states: "Robertson Macaulay's independent spirit was tested early. Adventurous by nature and fortified by the deep religious sentiment his mother had instilled, he began work at age 12 as a construction labourer at Stornoway, Scotland.

"Possessing only the rudiments of education but imbued

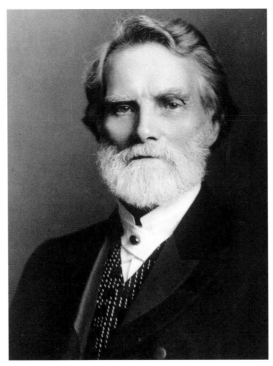

Above, Robertson Macaulay and right, Roderick Campbell – both learned lessons from their encounters with Donald Munro – and both went to Canada to put them into practice.

with the Scottish penchant for self-improvement, he devoted his evenings to unremitting study, concentrating on mathematics. He promptly secured an apprenticeship with the local solicitor and procurator fiscal. Macaulay's foray into law awakened his social conscience.

"As an officer of the court, he was obliged to evict crofters. The experience convinced him that economic security was the bedrock on which the well-being of families rested. The death of his father in 1847, when he was 14, cruelly reinforced this idea.

"Abandoning law, Macaulay worked briefly for the Hudson's Bay Company before venturing to Aberdeen, where he soon obtained a junior clerkship in the respected dry goods firm of Barker and Company. He remained for six years, but success did little to dampen his wanderlust. In 1854, at age 21, he set sail for Quebec."

David C. Boucher, who wrote the CDNB entry, believes the dedication to "personal integrity and social responsibility" which grew out of this experience with Munro's legal practice that underpinned his revolutionary approach to insurance. Contemporary sales techniques were often patently unethical and life insurance policies were riddled with escape clauses. But, says Boucher, Macaulay held steadfastly to the belief that life insurance was a trust. Latitude in interpreting claims, he maintained, should naturally favour policyholders. Later, at Sun Life, Macaulay's views were given concrete expression with the introduction of the "unconditional policy." Based on these principles, Sun Life grew to be one of the biggest companies in the world.

Munro met a very different end. He was replaced as Factor after the uproar and court case which followed the land distribution and legal issues associated with the Bernera Riot of 1874 and lived in a house on Lewis Street for 15 years. James Shaw Grant's mother remembered him shuffling along the street surrounded by little boys all shouting "Cuiridh mi às an fhearran thus – I'll take the land from you" which was his oft-repeated former threat to crofters. Munro would lunge back at his tormentors with his walking stick and shout back at them: "Put your feet in a bag and walk." When Munro died, on August 12, 1890, aged 81, of pulmonary congestion, his death was registered by William Ross who described himself merely as a "neighbour" rather than a relative. Munro left no estate.

Campaign for new mill fails after blaze

The destruction by fire on February 28, 1890 of the grain mill in Willowglen led to years of conflict between the Matheson estate and local crofters about the provision of milling facilities. The story of the blaze itself is told in The Scottish Highlander of Thursday March 4, 1890. It reported:

"At about 12 o'clock on Friday night, flames were observed issuing from the meal mill about a mile from Stornoway, tenanted by Mr. Maclennan, miller, and within twenty minutes from the time the alarm was given the Stornoway Fire Brigade, under Captain Anderson, was on the spot with their fire engine, which they had to drag behind them.

"It was seen, however, that the fire had gained complete mastery of the building, which was a three-storey one, and its contents of a very combustible nature. The fire engine was speedily set to work, manned by many willing hands who had gathered to the spot and a powerful stream of water, drawn from the mill dam, poured into the burning building, but all the efforts were of no avail, and at about three o'clock the fire engine was stopped. Mr Colin Maciver, blacksmith, rendered very efficient aid.

"The mill, which with the machinery was valued at about £2000, and belonged to Lady Matheson, was not insured, and neither were the effects of the tenant, who will be a sufferer by from £200 to £300. Several crofters who had sent their grain to be ground lost all their year's produce. The cause of the fire is not known."

The mill – called Latta's Mill after Mr John Latta who was killed there in an accident in 1834 – was fitted with the best equipment available at that time, according to contemporary reports. In mid-1849 it was described by Ordnance Survey researcher Corporal Daniel Sutherland as a "corn mill worked by water, built of stone, two stories high, slated and in good repair." He went on to say that it had been run by a Mr Latta but he had died at the beginning of 1849. "Since then, it has been carried on by his sister (Margaret, who died unmarried in 1868) who occupies the adjacent cottage. The mill is chiefly used for

Nestling amid winter snow in the woodlands in Willowglen, in Lews Castle Grounds, is the Stornoway Waterwheel visitor centre, declared open on Friday October 21, 2005. The mill, built on the site of Latta's Mill burned down in 1890, and with its wheel housed in the original pit, links the present day with the traditions of an era when crofters throughout the Islands grew crops which had to be processed by the local mills. It also looks forward by generating electricity for lighting on nearby paths.

grinding oats and barley and it was for a long time the leading one in the Island." Mr John Maclennan, who took over the lease (or tack) of the mill and its associated lands stretching up Willowglen in 1853, was the husband of Margaret Latta's niece Mary. It seems he was already at the mill with his family by 1851, operating under William Latta's lease.

In a letter dated 27 August 1817, Lady Seaforth, the owner of Lewis at the time, said that previous to the building of the mill in Willowglen by her father all the mills on Lewis were "wretched hovels." It is not clear what happened to the previous mill across the valley from the new structure. Lady Seaforth was referring to the horizontal or Norse mills of which more than 300 are recorded on Lewis alone. The modern view is that local people's barley grain of that era was processed by small scale technology well adapted to the contemporary scale of cultivation. At the time Lady Seaforth wrote, many landowners felt traditional small-scale production was holding back the community's economic development. The Willowglen Mill was one of four built by the Mackenzie landowners. The others were at Dell, Breasclete and Gress. Landowners derived revenue from their mills and people living in the surrounding area were thirled to their local mill – that is, they were obliged to use it to make their flour and pay for the privilege.

Lady Matheson became the sole proprietor of Lewis after the death of her husband Sir James in 1878. She held strong views on local development and its inpact on her visual amenity, to use the modern term. A minute of a meeting of the Stornoway Burgh Police Commissioners of July 1890 states that: "Lady Matheson declines to rebuild the Stornoway Mill, burnt down in March last: the want of the mill being a serious loss and inconvenience to the Parish of Stornoway." She later agreed to the building of a mill at Garrabost, opened in the mid-1890s, but the battle for the Stornoway mill went on. Over the years there were petitions to government offices, particularly the Congested Districts Board, in Edinburgh from various groups, the three main preferred locations being Garrabost itself, Lochs and a replacement for the Willowglen Mill.

In March 1897, the Highland News carried reports of a series of protest meetings held in Laxdale, Sandwick and other areas around the town about the problems caused by the lack of a mill. It was reported that the Landward Committee of Stornoway Parish Council had been in contact with the estate for six months about the matter, perhaps following the death of Lady Matheson in 1896, and Major Donald Matheson succeeding to the estate. A petition calling for a new mill was submitted in August 1896, just over four months after Lady Matheson died.

On March 6, 1897, it was reported in The Highland News that the Inspector of Poor in Stornoway had had to give temporary relief in the form of meal "in a few cases where the applicants had considerable quantities of grain on hand, but were unable to get it ground. This was despite the building of the mill at Garrabost three years earlier. A public meeting in Laxdale on February 26, 1897, heard from Alexander Morison, of Stornoway, as chair of the meeting, that crofters often lost five or six days waiting their turn because of having to go to mills in other districts to get their grain ground. "Without the mill their grain was of very little use to the crofters as they could only get from 1s 3d to 1s 6d per bushel for it in Stornoway, which meant a very serious loss."

Crofter Alexander Macdonald told the meeting about having to wait a week at the Gress mill to get 30 bushels of oats ground, while Mr Murdo Macdonald from Lochs told of crofters having to give their grain to the cattle while using the rent money to buy flour in from merchants. In reply, the view of the Matheson estate lawyers was that because there were two mills available (at Garrabost and Gress) "we think that no serious hardship is likely to arise through want of milling facilities." Mills were not needed in every township and building additional ones might "affect the efficiency of those already existing."

Protests continued, but a clear "No" from the estate came in 1899. The Congested Districts Board was based in Edinburgh and the Matheson lawyers/estate agents were Skene Edwards & Garson, also based in the city. On February 18, 1899, the board wrote to the lawyers to say "that various applications have been made to them for aid to erect a Meal Mill in the vicinity of Stornoway to supply the want caused by the burning of the old Mill in 1890. The Congested Districts Board would be obliged by your informing them if the Lewis Estate Management have considered the question of rebuilding or assisting in rebuilding the Mill at Stornoway, and if so, at what determination they have arrived."

A later letter from the Matheson lawyers makes clear the level of assistance which the Board was prepared to offer. On the 15th September 1899, the Matheson lawyers wrote to the Board: "We have received your letter of yesterday, enquiring whether Major Matheson would be prepared to build the mill at Stornoway and make due arrangements for its management and upkeep provided the Congested Districts Board should make a grant of 75 per cent. of the estimated cost of the mill with a limit of expenditure to be fixed after investigation."

The lawyers contacted Major Matheson and received a very dismissive response. In a letter to the Board on 19th September 1899, they wrote: "We have heard from Major Matheson, who states the mill which was burnt down did not pay, that the mill at Garrabost was intended to come in place of it, and that he does not think a new mill is required or that it would be expedient to proceed with the scheme." He therefore rejected the offer of a grant.

A further paragraph confirms that the location of the mill site in the Lews Castle Grounds was the main stumbling block for the Mathesons. The lawyers wrote: "Major Matheson does not, however, wish to put any obstacles in the way of the erection of a mill; and, if the promoters are satisfied that another mill is required, he is willing to give them such facilities as the law of entail permits him to give for the erection of a mill outside the policies [the Castle Grounds] at a moderate annual rent. Major Matheson would not sanction any arrangements under which any part of the cost, either of building or of working the mill, should be borne out of the rates."

Despite this response, the issue continued to be raised and the Highland News of January 27, 1917 reported a debate at Stornoway Parish Council in which it was reported that protests had been made about the state of the Gress Mill and in support of rebuilding the mill in Willowglen. The Board of Agriculture for Scotland had provided £80 towards a new mill wheel at Gress but no mention is made of a response about the town mill. So the campaign to restore the mill may only have ended with the Leverhulme purchase of Lewis in 1918. However, despite the passage of decades, not only did the original housing of the 19th century wheel survive to become part of the modern waterwheel, but also the mill lade and mill pool survived in the undergrowth and have been excavated, newly-lined and provided with a path. During construction a variety of other relics were found including a millstone.

South Beach, Stornoway, after the Great Storm in October 1882, with the barque Ellen left high and dry. In the distance on the left, the ruins of the old Castle are still visible. Along South Beach Street, there was first Carn House – where the gardens now are – then The Haven, followed by the Lewis Coffee Shop and the Star Inn. The timber strewn on the beach may have been from a cargo of wood intended for the construction of No 1 Pier – the cargo ship with this load lost half of it in the storm.

Developing the town's harbour

It was the development of harbour facilities in Stornoway in the last 50 years of the 19th century that drove the development of the town and the fishing industry in Lewis.

Landowner Sir James Matheson seemed to fail to recognise the potential for the fishing industry. His second factor or chamberlain, John Munro Mackenzie, made a reasoned argument for supporting fishing all round Lewis – saying that the money invested would produce a good return, benefiting both estate and people. But Sir James refused.

In Stornoway there had been haphazard development for centuries. In 1816, eight Stornoway traders collected money to repair and improve the 'old pier' on the end of the North Beach side of the harbour. They also formed a committee and drew up regulations to manage the quay and harbour; they appointed a harbourmaster with the approval of the then landlord, Lord Seaforth. They tried to constitute a proper harbour authority but nothing had been achieved by the time Mr James Matheson acquired the Island in 1844.

Matheson was certainly aware of the need to improve services to the mainland and he introduced the first regular steamboat service between Stornoway and the mainland, with regular improvements including the purchase of the Ondine in 1871. He also strengthened the island shipbuilding industry with the construction of the Patent Slip shipyard.

By 1860, Sir James was also the MP for the islands as part of the Ross and Cromarty constituency. As both MP and landowner, Sir James was the conduit for the continuing attempts to get statutory powers to run the harbour. However, without prior warning, he bought the rights to foreshores from the Lords Commissioners of the Treasury and promptly, through his factor Donald Munro, began to control and restrict activities around the harbour. The Foreshore Question then became the dominant local issue – and public meetings and petitions followed. Among those who signed the petition to Parliament were 16 fish curers, 13 coopers and 36 fishermen, indicating the extent of the fishing activity in Stornoway in the 1860s.

The end result of months of exchanges was the creation of the Stornoway Pier and Harbour Commission which first met in 1864. In June 1865 Stornoway Harbour Order received Royal Assent and relationships between the port and the estate improved so much that Sir James lent the capital for the first new wharves, extending over the west beach and in front of the steam boat wharf. The total cost of the work was just over £8000.

These very necessary improvements provided for the expansion of the fishing industry in Lewis in the 1860s and 1870s when the fishermen were getting larger fishing boats. Authority was sought in 1881 for the construction of an extension of 200 feet to No.1 Wharf, creating the original No 1 pier. Work took until 1883.

The 1865 plan

After that, there started a long battle with Sir James' widow, Lady Matheson, who was opposed to further harbour developments. Proposals to infill part of the harbour between the Patent Slip and Goat Island were refused. Lady Matheson had a particular objection to expansion of the herring curing stations. By 1887, the port was running out of space to accommodate all the boats trying to use the wharves. Lady Matheson continued to resist the proposals culminating in fiery public meeting in 1891 at which it was claimed she had "paralysed and crippled trade, especially in the kipper department of Stornoway which was the envy of the civilised world." It was January 1892 – after eight years of struggle between the Commissioners and the landowner – that Lady Matheson finally agreed to make the land available for expansion.

As a result solid quays were now constructed along Cromwell Street, North Beach and South Beach and this order gave authority to construct two more timber wharves which became known as No.2 and No.3 wharves, There was very considerable infilling to be carried out in the open spaces between the new solid quays and the existing roadways.

Eventually these reclaimed areas were invaluable because they provided essential space for the rapidly developing herring fishing industry, particularly the curing yards where thousands of barrels could be seen stacked up ready for the feverish activity of the fishing seasons. The Fish Mart was built in 1894 to serve the needs of the fishing fleets.

Further Harbour Orders followed in 1926 and 1947 which extended and strengthened the town wharves and finally linked Goat Island with the shore. In the 1970s the development of roll-on/roll-off ferries saw major changes to the port, including the demolition of the old Fish Mart. In the 1990s the new ferry terminal was built and opened.

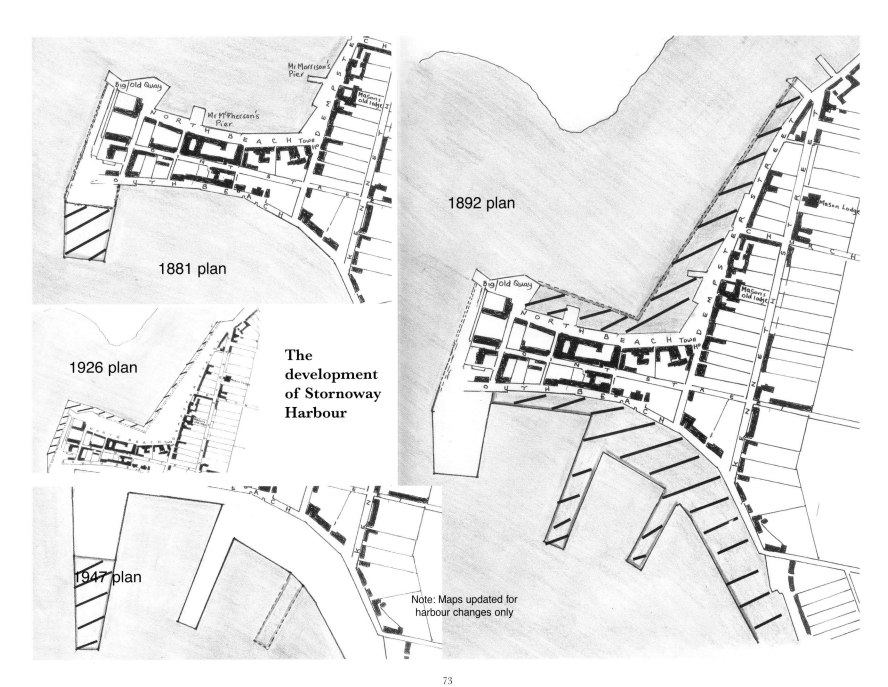

The
development
of Stornoway
Harbour

1881 plan

1892 plan

1926 plan

1947 plan

Note: Maps updated for harbour changes only

Coping with the impact of poverty

On 12th July 1893, representatives of the four parochial boards of Lewis met in 41 Kenneth Street, Stornoway. at the offices of the Stornoway Board, to draw up plans to build a poorhouse for the island. As a result, the Lewis Combination Poorhouse committee was formed under the initial chairmanship of Mr Charlie Orrock, the Chamberlain of the Lews at that time.

It was in 1895, after surveying several locations, that the poorhouse committee took over a site of about three acres from landowner Lady Matheson on part of Ropework Park, Coulregrein, with an annual rent of £3 per acre. Another acre of ground was acquired a few years later. The site was near the junction with the Laxdale to Goathill road (which is called Perceval Road today) on what is now known as Westview Terrace.

Construction of Coulregrein House took place in 1895-97 and cost £3,930, no less than £870 below the original estimate! Initially, 60 places were allocated at the new poorhouse; 30 to Stornoway and 10 each to the other three parishes. Within a year, this changed to 33 for Stornoway and 11 each for the others.

The cost of furnishing, maintenance and management was borne by the four parishes in respect of their allocated shares. They also agreed to bear, "the cost of boarding their own paupers with inmates thereof at the weekly rate which in due course shall be duly fixed." In 1910 the weekly rate was a shilling per inmate and 1s 3d for the sick.

The Lewis Combination Poorhouse was officially opened (ahead of schedule as well as under budget!) on 8th September 1897 by Major Donald Matheson, who was by then the proprietor of Lewis following Lady Matheson's death in 1896. The facility originally contained a laundry, kitchen, dining hall, a small infirmary, mortuary and separate dormitories for male and female inmates as well as children. There was also a large garden planted with cabbages, potatoes, turnips, oats and sometimes fruit such as strawberries. At various times the poorhouse also possessed horses, pigs, chickens and, for a time, a dairy cow.

The first inmates, admitted on 28th October 1897, were a 25-year-old unmarried fish worker and her son of less than a year old. The first Local Government Board inspection of the new poorhouse was published in June 1898. It stated: "The House is in excellent order and is now practically complete, and the arrangement of the House and accommodations is of a very high standard and will stand comparison with any poorhouse in Scotland." At the time of the inspection there were eight inmates, made up of five males, and three females although the building was approved to accommodate up to 34 people at this time.

In the early years, people who lived within three miles were allowed to visit Coulregrein House each Wednesday between 2.30 pm and 4.30 pm. Those from the country parishes had to seek permission from the Governor. Many inmates went to Coulregrein because of their health both physical and mental – there was little or no alternative provision for such people.

A report on the five years up to 1902 showed that over this time some 146 people were admitted. Three of the 1897 intake, four from 1898, one from 1899, two from 1900 and eight from 1901 were still in the house. Fourteen inmates had died.

The admissions register shows that 1,490 people, a figure that includes re-admissions, went into the institution between October 1st 1897 and December 1944. The totals are not recorded thereafter. The discharge register shows that most inmates left because their circumstances improved; they found work, went home or their health got better. Some left because they did not like the regime and were reported as 'absconded'. Inmates could leave at any time but many went back if things did not work out in the wider community.

The inmates were expected to work. The women generally performed domestic duties; the cleaning, the laundry and so on. They also knitted garments and made straw mats for sale. The men performed mainly physical work generally in the garden. In the late spring and summer months it was a familiar sight for locals to see a troop of grey uniformed men walking from Coulregrein House out to the moors to cut and take home the peats. The Board approved of this work because it cut down on the cost of buying coal.

For those who were judged to have worked hard in their allotted duties there was the reward of extra rations. Gifts of food from family, friends and neighbours were allowed for some but not for others, such as unmarried mothers. Tobacco was only allowed for the infirm or working males.

Occasionally the local authorities would approach the Board with a request that male inmates perform road repairs. Even those described as 'harmless lunatics' were expected to work. The inspector from the Board of Lunacy was of the view in 1906 that; "it is invariably found that much more efficient labour is obtained from lunatics than from ordinary inmates." The term harmless or temporary lunatic which is used frequently in the poorhouse records, often included people whom society today would categorise as experiencing depression, learning difficulties and other mental health problems.

The dietary routine remained broadly unchanged throughout the decades. Inmates were given bread, margarine and tea, for breakfast at 8am. Dinner at noon consisted of soup or broth and fish (herring) or meat with potatoes and tea on alternate days. Tea was served at 3pm and supper, which consisted of porridge and milk, at 8.30pm . At weekends, there was bread, cheese and tea for breakfast plus rice or pea soup with meat and potatoes for lunch.

As with other poorhouses elsewhere, Coulregrein House also took in children. Younger children were accommodated with their mothers. Older children and orphans were placed in the children's ward. There were a few sad cases of children who had been 'deserted by parents'. Children could stay in the poorhouse until they were 16, then they were classed as adults. A few were fortunate to be taken in by a family member, friend or neighbour. Some were adopted.

Like their contemporaries out in the wider community, Poorhouse children had to attend school. The punishment book records one case of 'skiving' from school by a boy

The gateway and Governor's House in Westview Terrace, above, are all that remains of the Poorhouse and its grounds, pictured right

inmate for which he received three strokes of the Governor's strap.

The children of sick parents were sometimes admitted. At a time when tuberculosis was endemic in Lewis and elsewhere, parents on the poor roll or sick poor roll might be sent to the Mossend Fever Hospital or the Sanatorium [that is the old County Hospital which was on the site of the present Glen Seillach Business Park] to recover whilst their children were looked after in the poorhouse. There were sometimes entire families lodged at Coulregrein. The death of a parent or parents, desertion, alcoholism or the inability of relatives or friends to support them were among the more common causes for admission of family groups.

The poorhouse sick roll shows a typical spread of the more common illnesses including: various ailments of old age and mental health problems. The roll also has frequent references to alcoholic cases. More serious medical cases

were transferred to the care of the Lewis Hospital, which was not far away Goathill Road and was replaced, like the County Hospital, in the early 1990s by the Western Isles Hospital.

However, the hospital also had to make space for more urgent cases. "The Poor Law Infirmary with its inadequate nursing staff and equipment make one hesitate before transferring a patient." says the 1927 annual report of the Lewis Hospital. To save on costs the Board had employed temporary and unqualified nursing staff despite constant pleas for improvements from the medical officer.

As a result of local government reforms which came into force in 1929, Ross and Cromarty County Council and the town council took over the responsibility for Poor Law administration. In May 1930 a new sub-committee was established to oversee the running of the poorhouse. One of the first acts of the new committee was to change its

official name to Coulregrein House.

By 1946 the ground floor wards, made up of 2 to 10 beds each, were considerably overcrowded according to official reports. There were a total of 72 beds in the institution at this time. Of this number 25 were set aside for the chronically sick and another two for maternity cases.

With the introduction of the National Health Service in 1948, the old Poor Laws were finally swept away. The way of life at Coulregrein slowly changed from that of a Poor Law institution to a residential home.

However, Coulregrein House remained 'Tigh nam Bochd' to generations of Stornowegians until it was demolished in 1980 – not surprisingly without any protests or regrets. All that remains now of the Victorian structures are the Governor's House and main entrance gateway on Westview Terrace.

In September 1902, Stornoway was visited by King Edward VII and Queen Alexandra, the first reigning monarch to visit the town since James V in 1540. The Coronation had been held in London on August 9, having been delayed because the King was seriously ill. The new King was almost 60 at the time of the death of his mother Queen Victoria in 1901. The drawing shows the Royal Couple leaving Cuddy Point and comes from the van der Werff family, descendants of the Mathesons. Peggy, one of Major Duncan Matheson's children, is remembered in the family as having been unimpressed with all the pomp and circumstance – she recalled that she just wanted to escape and climb trees with her brother Kildare.

Above the first Town Hall after its opening in 1905

Left, an admission card to the original opening ceremony, and, right, views of the burned-out shell in 1918

Double disaster in Stornoway as a major storm floods the town centre and brings down more of the ruined Town Hall

Burning out the heart of the town

On Saturday March 2, 1918, the proud civic heart of Stornoway was destroyed in little more than two hours. The municipal offices were entirely gutted by fire. The Stornoway Gazette reported: "Stornoway's Town Hall, Public Library, and Municipal Offices – the whole magnificent pile – was totally destroyed by fire on Saturday. That announcement will be sad news for Lewis folk in all parts of the world just as the ruin is a melancholy spectacle for those of us at home."

Lost were the Lewis Estate offices; the entire public library and almost all its stock of books; the offices of the Lochs and Barvas Parish Councils; the offices of the Lewis District Council, and the district surveyor and sanitary inspector. Also destroyed were the Town Clerk's office as well as that of the Pier and Harbour Commission and ex-Provost Anderson's law offices. The public space of the Town Hall was also gone – indeed, the third floor of the building was lost forever as it was not replaced in the later reconstruction.

The building had been used by the Royal Navy during the war and the fire was discovered by the Fleet Paymaster whose offices overlooked South Beach. . The fire became a furnace after it spread to the Town Hall itself which was gaslit by 12 large chandeliers. The fire ate its way up the gas pipes and set the roof ablaze.

This blaze seemed to form part of a black pattern of disaster coming during the last year of the Great War in which more than 1,000 Lewisman were killed and many more injured – and being followed only 10 months later by the Iolaire disaster that claimed more than 200 lives when the troopship was wrecked on the Beasts of Holm.

The impact of the losses in the First World War cannot be exaggerated. The total population of Lewis, between 1914-18, was approximately 30,000. From this, the island contributed about 6,200 servicemen (including returning emigrants) to the war effort. Consequently, about 20 per cent of the entire Lewis population was on active service in some capacity during World War One with approximately

The official party at the opening of the first Town Hall

half of them serving in the Royal Naval Reserve (RNR).

It was not until Wednesday June 19, 1929, that Stornoway's second Town Hall was officially opened with great ceremony. The long delay in reconstruction after the devastating fire in 1918 was the result of a number of factors. Lord Leverhulme, who owned Lewis at the time, had major plans to redevelop Stornoway which included a completely new civic centre. Progress could only be made after this plan was dropped four years later.

In addition, there were outstanding debts of £1338 relating to the building of the original Town Hall. It had cost £11,500 to build. There was also the need to raise money because, as prices soared in the aftermath of the Great War, the rebuilding costs greatly exceeded the insurance paid out on the old building. This was a time of great economic hardship on the Islands as thousands had left for the Dominions on emigrant ships.

To the rescue from Canada and America came several

people with Island links who donated considerable sums of money to rebuild the Town Hall, re-equip the Library (which was provided with a specially fireproofed area) and even added an up-to-date fire engine to the local fleet.

The funds came from Mr T. B. Macaulay, who had succeeded his father Robertson as President of the Sun Life Assurance company of Canada; Mr John Bain of Chicago; Mr William Macaskill; and others as well as money raised locally. These benefactors had been generous in support of other ventures as well. The new buildings – including the library and books – cost £25,000 of which £11,400 came from the insurance payout and rest from fund-raising. Including the value of the foundations and the original walls included in the new building, it was reckoned the new Town Hall and offices were worth £35,000 at 1929 prices.

The foundation stone of the first Town Hall was laid on August 12, 1903, and the building was opened on September 7, 1905. At the first of these events, Major Matheson, then owner of Lewis, said: "This building is the heart, the brain, the centre of the common life of the people of the island. Stornoway is not the Lews, but it must needs be its centre, and this building represents the head of the body politic, where is concentrated all its corporate vitality."

Construction of the £11,500 building was assisted by £3500 towards the library from Dr Carnegie; and more than £2000 from the Coats family in Paisley. Guest of honour at the opening was former prime minister and foreign secretary Lord Rosebery; guests included the Earl and Countess of Glasgow and Gerald Balfour, the MP for Leeds and President of the Board of Trade.

The scene on Armistice Day in November 1918 as the Great War came to an end with Stornoway base commander Admiral Boyle addressing crowds of servicemen and civilians in front of the former Imperial Hotel (later the Louise Carnegie Hostel). Behind Admiral Boyle is Provost Murdo Maclean (with chain of office). Only weeks later, in the early hours of January 1, 1919, Admiral Boyle and the community as a whole would confront the Iolaire tragedy which cost so many Island servicemen's lives after the War itself had ended.

Left, Cromwell Street in the late 1920s; above, tree-cutting in Perceval Square as the road is widened in 1971; and, below, a watery time at Lazy Corner in November 1959

Over the years … clockwise from top left, the Castle Grounds with World War Two buildings on the Castle Green; the view from the new War Memorial; the Sail Loft before World War One; and Creed Mouth cottage about 100 years ago

When Hollywood came to Lewis...

'Going to the flicks' was a phrase once commonly heard on the streets of Stornoway. Between 1916 and 1977 cinema entertainment was a permanent fixture in the lives of people on Lewis, with the establishment of first the Lewis Picture House and then the Playhouse.

However, cinema entertainment in Stornoway began as early as 1898/99. A Lewis Hospital Report dated November 30 1899 shows that the proceeds of cinematograph entertainment for that year came to £18 3s 0d.

The first proper picture house was established on Keith Street prior to the First World War but its eventual demise was only months later when it was destroyed by fire. Its replacement continued to grow in stature. Completed and opened in May 1916 the Lewis Picture House soon engrossed the imaginations of children and adults alike. In his article 'When Hollywood came to Lewis', Stornoway Gazette owner and editor James Shaw Grant reminisced about the early years of the picture house.

"The arrival of cinema altered our boyish lives. . . The attraction [for us] was the serial rather than the feature picture ... always, I left the cinema in a state of apprehension, with my hero lying on the rails before an oncoming train, or tied to a tree with a score of Indians aiming arrows at his heart."

The cinema played a huge part in the social structure of the town, creating an alternative form of entertainment and allowing people a glimpse at the wacky world of Hollywood and the magic and mystery which was being created there.

A press cutting dated September 15,1921 states: 'Under the experienced management of Mr A..B. Blair, the Lewis Picture House continues to gain favour as a place of entertainment. Since coming to Stornoway, he has laid himself out to study the public taste, and he never fails to provide a first class programme. The result is seen in the steady increase in regular patrons, who appreciate the general manager's efforts to cater for them."

The Lewis Picture House premises could be found at the

"Laugh and the World laughs with you; stay out and feel miserable alone."

ENJOY NATURE'S MEDICINE BY MAKING A POINT OF VISITING

THE

LEWIS PICTURE HOUSE

KEITH STREET,

STORNOWAY.

DOSES GIVEN FRESH EVERY

MONDAY. WEDNESDAY, AND FRIDAY, AT 7 P.M.

POPULAR PRICES:

4d, 7d, 11d, (Reserved) 1s 2d.

From one of the first editions of the Stornoway Gazette, January 19th 1917

Lewis Street end of Keith Street, the opposite end to where the original picture house had once stood, beside what was once Lady Matheson's Female Industrial School. The cinema had no balcony and sloped fairly steeply from the cushioned rear seats (2/4d for adults, 9d for children) to "the hard bench seats for the plebs" (Alan Campbell's *Memories of a Kenneth Street Boy*). In one of the first editions of the Stornoway Gazette, January 19 1917, an advertisement for the picture house describes its menu of comedy films as 'nature's medicine' and at the height of the First World War this must really have been the case.

These first movies were silent, showing the hilarious antics of the likes of Charlie Chaplin and Laurel and Hardy, but Christmas Day 1930 saw the arrival of the talkies in Stornoway. Under the expert supervision of Will Mack modifications were made to the Picture House including the installation of a sound system and a false ceiling to trap the sound. Will Mack became the owner of the Picture House on November 5, 1925 with combined roles of 'director, cinema proprietor, projectionist, actor-manager, singer, dancer and general entertainer' (*Practical Family History December 2002, 'Will Mack*: by Donald Mack').

Unfortunately, insufficient revenue and a building which was rapidly falling into disrepair forced Mack to sell. Stornoway Playhouse Ltd (part of a chain of cinemas owned by a Dundee based company) purchased the premises and in June 1933 the Picture House opened newly refurbished under the new management of General Manager J B Milne.

However, this was just a temporary measure. On November 10, 1933, Stornoway Playhouse Ltd announced its share issue along with an artist's impression of what the proposed purpose-built cinema would look like. In their prospectus giving details of the proposal it was stated that: 'The Directors are confident that there is a widespread demand in Stornoway for a modern and well-equipped picture house. There has been acquired on behalf of the Company the existing small picture house known as the "The Lewis Picture House".

The prospectus continued: "The Directors anticipate that they will be able to dispose of the building at a price approximating what was paid for it. By acquiring this existing picture house with its goodwill, they have reduced the possibility of uneconomic competition to a minimum. This, it is considered, ought to be an important factor towards the success of the Company."

Work progressed rapidly and on Monday 29, January, 1934, the Playhouse was officially opened by Viscount Tarbat of Castle Leod to a showing of 'Tell Me Tonight' starring Jan Kiepura. In the run up to the opening, the Playhouse building became the hot topic of conversation

"It is hardly necessary to emphasise the handsome appearance of the building, or the lavishness of the internal decorations. Many people have taken the opportunity recently of 'peeping' inside to see how the work was progressing. Placed at the corner of South Beach Street and Kenneth Street, the Playhouse occupies one of the most prominent feus in the town. On each side of the wide entrance hall of the Playhouse there is an up-to-date shop for the convenience of patrons, while in the hall itself stands the symbol of modernity – an automatic ticket machine." (*Stornoway Gazette*, January 26 1934)

Buses carrying private parties from nearly every part of the Island, including Tarbert and South Harris, were provided for the opening ceremony. Such was the grandeur of the event, the Viscount was piped from the Caledonian Hotel to the Playhouse by the Lewis Pipe Band.

The overwhelming success of the Playhouse continued to grow and in 1946 a record 4,000 people from all over the Island visited the Playhouse on Friday 23 and Saturday 24, August, 1946 to see the film "I Know Where I'm Going". This was a romance from the British-based film-makers Michael Powell and Emeric Pressburger. It starred Wendy Hiller and Roger Livesey, and featured Pamela Brown, Finlay Currie and Petula Clark in her fourth film appearance. With external scenes shot around the Isle of Jura, the film had the additional interest of including Murdo Morrison, a son of the Islands, in its cast. He spoke of the "colossal amount of romance to be found in the Highlands, if only we look for it, used our imagination, and took pride in our traditions…If we are going to have more films about the islands, we must not be too ready to find fault."

Cinema became an antidote to everyday life, an incredible world that seemed so real yet so fantastical. In an article '*Going to the Movies*', Angus McCormack reminisced on his visits to the cinema in the 1960s and the effect which it had over its viewers: "Cowboy movies were a favourite

and when the 'cavalry' rode in to the rescue the cheers would lift the roof … I recall on one occasion when the baddie was creeping up on an unsuspecting goodie, the whole theatre was on its feet shouting: 'He's behind you!"

In its final year the cinema began to come under scrutiny over the types of films being shown. At the same time, Kingsway Entertainment, the company which by then was the owner of the Playhouse, lacked the money and the enthusiasm to maintain the cinema, and the once modern high tech equipment began to fail to impress.

To make matters worse, July 1976 saw the arrival of colour television in Stornoway, and the trance with which cinema had once held people was broken. Sadly, almost exactly 43 years after its grand opening ceremony on January 29, 1934, the Playhouse was to close. After a short-lived battle against regulations and ultimately the church, the Stornoway Gazette on January 15, 1977 printed the Playhouse advert in its usual place on page two, with the sombre message: "Cinema Patrons Please Note: Due to unforeseen circumstances, it is regretted that this cinema will remain closed until further notice"

The Playhouse had for some time held bingo two nights a week and it continued as a bingo hall still under the management of Mr Duncan Mackinnon, until 1979 when it was bought over by local business man Colin Macaskill. May 14, 1979 saw the Playhouse reopened with a showing of 'The Thirty Nine Steps'. However, its revival was short-lived, and under increasing pressure regarding the fire regulations that had led to the Playhouse's earlier demise, Mr Macaskill sold the property to its current owners, the Royal British Legion.

So ended an epic tale in Stornoway's cinema history. What was once the projection room is now better known as the Crow's Nest, and the faces of the old greats, the action of the Cowboys and Indians, and the romance of Hollywood at its best, are now just memories within the old walls. As the years passed, showings organised by the Lewis Film Society kept the idea of local cinema alive – then came the publicly-funded Screen Machine in town centre car parks and later Filmobile Scotland with showings in the Town Hall. Finally, in late 2005, the purpose-built An Lanntair Arts Centre opened across the road from the former Playhouse and cinema productions became available again on a regular basis in its multi-role theatre.

The Playhouse dominates South Beach in this image from August 1945

A guide to Stornoway words from the 20th century

Compiled by Norman M Macdonald

A' Heerie	Exclamation of surprise
AP	Appointment, date
Aaa-ah-ooh	Loud yell, peculiar to Stornoway
Affa	Tail-end of a cigarette
Ah Giy	Behold
An Tigh Mor	The Poor House
Article	Useless person
Bachells	Boots
Bachles	Boots
Backsheds	Bells Road
Bankers	Field where Dun Berisay is built
Betsack	East Coast fisher lass
Billingsgate	Fishselling quay
Blartica	Kick it hard
Blone	A female, or your mother
Blooter	Obliterate
Blue Mogganer	Cove from Peterhead
Bootica	Boot it
Brammar	Lover
Brew	Old man
Brigade	Sea Cadets
Brockie	Cove from Fraserburgh
Brollocks	Shellfish
Bugle	Squeal, complain
Bumming	Telling lies
Burl	Spin in a car
Burma Road	Lower part of Smith Avenue
Canvastowner	Cove from Lower Sandwick
Cara	Bream
Carait	Pair of anything
Caravanoch	Red bream
Catta Bulka	Game played with a stick and a small four-sided and numbered piece of wood
Chow	Tobacco
Clawait	W. C.
Closter	Blow
Clown	Foolish person
Cob, the	The Cockle ebb
Colony	Weaving sheds at Cannery Road
Cooee	Greeting call
Coolivikish	Something secret
Cope	Dump, as a cart
Corner Boy	Young man about town
Country	Beyond the town
Cove	Male person
Cove from away	Incomer
Cox	Collide

Crab	Resident of Newton
Crack (1)	A good time
Crack (2)	What's the crack – what's happening
Crotan	Resident of the Battery
Crusty's Quay	Inner Harbour
Cu	Nasty piece of work
Cuddy	Young Pollock or saithe
Cuddy Point	Launching slip below the Castle
Dallag	Spotted dogfish
Dame	Female person
Dan Dougal's Brae	Brae at Western Isles Hospital
Deasoch	Boat, or man, from mainland west coast
Deng	Blast it (exclamation)
Deuk	Duck (the head)
Dode	Cove from Buckie
Dooker	Scart or Cormorant
Dosh	Money
Dossan	Fringe of hair on forehead
Down the Vile	Down the town
Dry Land Sailors	Sea Cadets
Duish (1)	Gurgling sound, washing
Duish (2)	Stout, blubberly sort of cove
Eelie	Trawler
Essing	Skulking (playing truant)
Fillag	Seagull
Flakers	Fallen, in drink
Flanker	A fast one (pulling a)
Fleured	Plastered
Flicks	The cinema
Fluke	Small flatfish
For nasky	Free
Fore-and-after	Sailing ship cove
Fuchled	Done out, exhausted
Fullaster	Full speed
Geehonk	Drunkard, idiot

Geehow	Foolish person
Geely	Pool at Tong Sands
Gelley	Fire
Gensey	Jersey
Gissa	Give me
Give Less	Stop it
Glockeehaw	Guileless sort of bloke
Goak	April Fool
Gock	Tap
Gorra	Have you got?
Gossar	Any particularly interesting thing
Graisg	Hoi polloi (the masses, the common people)
Green Island	Small islet adjoining Goat Island
Grespan	Cheeky youngster
Gribbon	A nuisance of a small boy
Grounds	Lady Lever Park
Grubber	Lewis Poor House
Gullack	Seagull
Gut House	Fish processing factory
Haler	I choose
Heilars	I bags
Heng	Oh Heng! (exclamation)
Hengoes	Variation of 'heng'
High Road	Road in Grounds
Hoil	The harbour water
Hoaching	Crawling
Hoof	To pinch something and run
Hookit	Run away, from thugad
Hurl	A ride in a vehicle
Hurley	Two-wheeled barrow or handcart
Hurrow	Hullo
Kady	Cap
Kail Eyed	Intoxicated, Int't there
Kayock	Cove from Sutherland
Keehow	A bit of a lad or an unpredictable cove
Keeswasterer	Swinging blow to the body
Kennethed	Arrested
Kibosh	Celp bais, black cap
Knockan	A drink
Koalie	Louse
Lairy	Foolish
Lap	Person from Coulregrein
Lapag	Useless woman
Lavvy Brushes	Life Boys
Lazy Corner	Inner Harbour, North Beach

Lornes	Type of shoe
Lourag	Female from the country
Lourak	Happy country gentleman
Low Road	Road in Grounds
Lowback	Flounder
Mackatuin	Nonsense
Maggie's	A sweetshop on Castle Street (Maggie York's)
Maori	Someone from out of town
Masher	Just pretend
Maw	Person from the countryside
Mask	Halfpenny
Meppan	Brat
Meppan Show	Puppet
Mog	Mackerel
Mogareel	Scandinavian Seaman
Moocher	Scrounger
Mookun	Tin jug used for beer in a bothan
Morning	First drink of the day
Narrows	Cromwell Street Narrows
Neaff	Annoying person
Neb	Nose
Tin School, Wee School, Clock School	The Nicolson Institute (or parts of)
No empty	Well off
No great	Not friends
Not worth	No good
Number Seven	Area behind Arnish Lighthouse
Ocroch	Town tip
Oh-Dhee-Ah	Expression of disgust
Old Laid	Mother
Old Man	Father
Ollack	A stone
Oolpack	Large stone
Opera House	Public toilet
Outer	Throw-in at football
Pallack	Porpoise
Partyvella	Joyful social gathering
Peederandick	Home made toy which clicks
Plastered	Drunk
Plo-tan	Grassy peat used for roll-up cigarettes
Pooch	Pocket
Pooley	The Plantation
Poy Oy	Post Office
Privy	WC
Pulley	Plantation
Push	Opt out
Putting Past	Saving
Pyags	Plenty
On the Tack	Off the alcohol
Queen Steps	Steps on King Edward Wharf
Raggans	Temper (in the raggans)
Rance	A bar, eg on a chair
Raut	Yarn, long story
Scart	Cormorant
Scloosh	Mud or similar
Sclotack	Small fish, whiting
Scoorie	Seagull
Scorp	Country cove
Scran	Uber (see under U) you feel you have a vague right to
Scroobie	School janitor, whipper-in of skulkers
Scrope	Mark with the fingernails
Scrub	Outwith town limits (Sandwick, Laxdale, etc)
Scutt	Plastered
Sglog	Blow
Sgroig	A pipe
Shellback	Sailing ship cove
Shiantak	Clout, especially to the gob (mouth)
Shinedag	Hefty blow
Shmealak	Backhanded blow to the dial (face)
Shoogly	Shaky
Shot	A fair amount of alcohol
Show me	Give me
Sillshin	Having a high opinion of oneself
Sim's Clock	Town Hall Clock
Sked	Herring
Skemp	A show-off
Skian off	Run away
Sklundeag	A spit
Skulk	Play truant
Skuteil	Play in water or mud
Slider	Ice cream wafer
Slog	Powerful kick
Slope	Policeman
Sloshed	Inebriated
Smeg	Smoke
Smeggan, a	Slightly tipsy
Smellack	Hard blow
Smookers	Small amounts, dregs, scarpings
Smoote	A good glow on
Sneachie	Steal
Snebbie	A card game in which the loser gets flicked across the nose with playing cards
Sober Island	Small island opposite the freight ferry terminal
Spart a Vento	Newton
Spaultrack	A split herring
Spoch	To squirt
Spoey	Cat
Spunyan	Rope
Sqeggie	Person or eyes with a squint
Stoker	Baksheesh (money given as a tip)
Stornoway Wire	Specific whistle only identified by Stornoway coves
Strak	Stroke of the tawse (leather strap)
Straveking	Late evening walkabout to Cromwell Street
Stroop	Noise made when eating soup
Strupag	Cup of tea
Susnoch	Scandinavian expression
Sull	Pollock fish
Sullack	Young codfish
Swipe	Steal
Taoming	A thrashing
Tarrygassed	Sherbet fountain
The Day	Today
Thon	Of recent memory
Tool	Foolish person
Toss	Take a fall
Troc	Worthless person
Tweeze	To inform on
Twid	Having told on
Twig	To understand, to figure out (tuig)
Uber	To steal, something stolen
Ulster	Ulcer
Vile, the	Town
Wee Marag	Small fat person
Well Oiled	Drunk
Whipper-in	Truant Officer
Whurry	Salt boat
Wing	Penny
Works	A thrashing

The picture to the top left is a view of Cromwell Street during the visit of Edward VII in 1902: bottom left is Perceval Square during the events to mark the Coronation of George V in 1911; above the same location for the Coronation of George VI in 1937; and then below, the scene for the Coronation of Elizabeth II in 1953.

"It was after six o' clock when the "Metagama" weighed anchor, and it will be a lasting memory for those who witnessed the scene as the huge ocean greyhound and the small coaster parted company, and the voyagers on the top decks of the great liner exchanged farewells with relatives and chums on the deck of the "Hebrides," the pipe band the while playing "The Road to the Isles"

Piped along the quay …

…music as they start the trip out to the Metagama

Off to Canada!

Saturday April 21, 1923 saw the departure of the liner Metagama to Canada carrying around 300 people all but 20 of whom were young men, hoping to find a better life abroad than in Lewis where the economic crisis which followed World War One had bitten deep, particularly after the ending of the development schemes backed by Lord Leverhulme. The Friday night before Metagama Day had seen the town packed with people, waiting to leave, and waiting to say goodbye. Then the liner dropped anchor out in the harbour. As with other emigrant ships like the Marloch, which had left the Islands the week before, the migrants had to head off from the Stornoway harbour quays on board coasters, like the Glendun. The size of the passenger liners meant they were unable to come alongside in Stornoway or at other island harbours. According to reports, few of the parents made their way to the pier – private goodbyes had been said at home beforehand.

Crowds packed No 1 Pier as the coaster pulled away … off shore lay the Metagama, seen below

Above, the Lews Castle conservatories seen in the 1930s

Right, A view down Cromwell Street from outside the Town Hall in June 1959 with the Neptune Bar on the right.

A miscellany of Stornoway II

■ The Highland News of 30th December 1905 reported "Christmas Day passed off almost unobserved in Stornoway. The schools, banks and public offices were closed for the day, which was also observed as a holiday of the Naval Reserve Battery. Otherwise the business of the town went on as usual. The weather for sometime back has been exceedingly wet and stormy, but on Christmas a delightful change was experienced. A keen frost set in on Sunday night, rendering the previously muddy roads firm under foot. This coupled with the bright sunshine and bracing atmosphere, made walking in the Castle Grounds exceedingly pleasant for those at liberty to enjoy it. The members of the Good Templar Lodge celebrated the day with a very enjoyable social in the evening, which took the place of the usual meeting. The seasonal traffic at the Post-Office was as heavy as ever, but extra accommodation was had in the Social Institute, North Beach, and the officials were thus able to cope more successfully with the rush." [The local Good Templar Lodge was a temperance organisation, part of a high-profile national campaign to eradicate alcohol misuse through good morals and abstinence. The Post Office was then emporarily located in the Town Hall, after moving from its old premises in Perceval Square. In 1908, 'the Poy-Oy' moved into new purpose-built premises in Francis Street where it remains to this day.]

■ Lewis proprietor James Matheson commissioned the building of the *Mary Jane*, an iron-hulled paddle steamer named in honour of his wife following their marriage in November 1843. The vessel at first served as his own yacht and first came into use in 1846, having been built at the Tod & MacGregor shipyard in Glasgow. The *Mary Jane* was soon being used to transport people to and from the mainland and in 1851 she was sold to the Glasgow and Lochfyne Steam Packet Company and used on its Inverary service. In 1875 the vessel was lengthened, her original clipper bow was replaced with a gently raked stem, and she was renamed the Glencoe. As such, she continued in service until 1931,

becoming the oldest steamship in use in the world – although she was reboilered twice, the original steeple engine (so-called because the piston rod extension looked like a church tower) remained in use throughout. She was broken up in Ardossan in 1931, after 85 years of service.

■ The oil-fired power station on Battery Point was built after the Second World War, adjacent to existing wartime oil storage tanks, and now supplies power only when the mainland link is unavailable. This is on part of the site of what was the UK's biggest Royal Naval Reserve base and battery from 1876 until 1919 when it was shut in naval cutbacks after the First World War.

■ From the early1830s a whisky distillery stood on the site now occupied by the Sawmill Woodland Centre in Lews Castle Grounds. It was described as being on "a grand scale, with coppers of large diameter, furnaces, vats, coolers, flake-stands under a running stream; also a very large malt-barn and mill." It was said to be of the most modern design, and had its own quay. It was part of a concerted effort to stop illicit private distilling of usquebagh (whisky) or the even stronger tres-tarig which the Customs and Excise were anxious to stop – for reasons of revenue rather than social concerns. On June 25, 1833, Alex Stewart, factor of Lewis, reported that the distillery was "doing well". In 1840 it was seen as a suitable destination for a school trip from Uig. In 1851 Sir James Matheson's Chamberlain John Munro Mackenzie was looking for another site for the works. The distillery was demolished in 1857.

■ Beyond Arnish, on a hill beside the sea, is a monument to Prince Charles Edward Stuart which was put up in 1904. In 1746, following his defeat at the Battle of Culloden, the fugitive prince was briefly kept hidden in a house which stood on a hillside removed in the 1970s to create the Arnish oil fabrication yard. In a long article in the Celtic Monthly of 1904, Major Duncan Matheson, then owner of Lewis, told how on April 29, 1746 the Prince was in Scalpay, Harris, before heading north. Driven by a storm, he landed

near the head of Loch Seaforth, and walked "over moor and morass" to Stornoway. It was not till noon next day, May 5, that the Prince and his handful of companions reached Arnish Loch "all wet to the skin." The Prince had hoped to hire a boat in Stornoway but suspicions were aroused and local people requested that he should not get them into trouble by remaining in the island. However, "not one in Stornoway, rich or poor, made any attempt to secure the £30,000 that was waiting for them at Arnish." That was the Government's price on the Prince's head. At Kildun House, (later Arnish farm house), he was hospitably received by the Lady Kildun, a cousin of the anti-Jacobite landowner, Lord Seaforth. He dried his clothes at the fire, did a little amateur cooking and then went to bed for a much-needed rest. Early next morning, May 6th, the party embarked in a small boat and, plentifully supplied with provisions by their hostess, steered south. Alarmed by cruisers in the Minch, they slipped into Loch Shell, and spent four miserable days on Eilean Iubhard, sheltering as best they could in a roofless hut, the remains of which could still be seen in 1904. Thence he fled to Benbecula, to Skye and back to France.

■ After construction work which started in 1948 and was completed in 1954, Goat Island was linked to the Lewis shore in Newton by a causeway, realising an idea first suggested during the expansion of the harbour wharves in the 1880s. Goat Island has the only ship repair slipway of any size on the west coast of Scotland north of the Clyde. In earlier times it may have been fortified – the Cromwellian records from 1653 certainly refer to a fort on an island offshore. The name has nothing to do with goats – it may have been derived from the Gaelic words for windy or airy, or the word for spume, that is, the froth off waves. Goat Island was originally named Eilean Couill after a son of Somerled mac Gillebride, King of the Hebrides and of Kintyre, who was part Norse, part Gael and who wrested the area from King Godred of Man in two naval actions in the 12th century.

A view of central Stornoway from the air in June 1959 – © The Scotsman Publications Ltd. Licensor www.scran.co.uk

A town for tweed!

The Scottish Home Industries Association, one of the benevolent agencies set up to help island weavers, was established in 1889 and set up a depot in Cromwell Street, Stornoway – in addition to one in Tarbert and others in London and Edinburgh – to distribute the tweed.

The depots' establishment followed the shift, in the last 20 years of the nineteenth century, away from the selling of the tweed by members of the gentry towards a more commercial situation, with local merchants beginning to start dealing in the tweeds.

Near the end of the century, the Scottish Home Industries Association appointed an inspector, whose job it was to travel the isles with the aim of checking the quality of tweed being produced. In 1898 an instruction scheme was set up in Lewis, this time set up by the Congested Districts Board.

In 1903, Aeneas MacKenzie started the Patent Slip Carding Mill – so named because it was sited on the old boatbuilding slip.. The Patent Slip Mill was the predecessor of S.A. Newall and Sons Ltd and, in 1908, it expanded to include spinning facilities and keep up with the competition - Kenneth MacKenzie having set up a rival carding and spinning mill in 1906. Both businesses would have hoped they could attract some of the work which had been going to spinners on the mainland.

Aeneas MacKenzie went bust in 1910, at which point ownership of the slip mill passed into the hands of a Mr Morrison. It then went to an associate firm of Newalls in 1918, before coming into their direct ownership. In time, Kenneth MacKenzie's would move from Lewis Street to Seaforth Road.

Between 1903 and 1905 in Lewis, the value of tweed sales grew from £8000 to £20,460. Such a rate of growth led to doubts over the "legitimacy" of the process, with many believing the boom had been fuelled by increased use of millspun yarn. This increased output was linked with poorer weaving and a diminished respect for the industry in London, where the term "Stornoway tweeds" was coined for those made in Lewis. The SHIA's depots in Lewis were shut down as there was not sufficient handspun tweed around to justify the costs in keeping them open.

In 1906, a meeting was held in Stornoway by dealers in homemade tweed about the need for some type of tweed guarantee – moves that would eventually result in the Orb trademark. In 1909, the Harris Tweed Association was incorporated. They also applied to have an inspector based on the island, to apply the Orb stamp to tweeds which conformed to the trademark definition.

By 1910, the local mills had installed spinning machinery. But the merchants, who wanted to exclude millspun yarn, could not be too direct in their opposition as they still needed the mills to card wool for them.

Lord Leverhulme, who bought the Isle of Lewis in 1918, favoured millspinning and, in 1919, bought two-thirds of Kenneth MacKenzie Ltd. Later, he bought the rest of the company. Under his control, the business openly admitted using millspun yarn in their tweeds. Leverhulme also attempted to buy Newalls, but was refused. Leverhulme then gave up his Lewis schemes and the MacKenzie family bought back his entire shareholding in Kenneth MacKenzie Ltd.

In 1928 the Harris Tweed Association threatened both mills with legal action unless they stopped selling tweed made from millspun yarn as Harris Tweed. It became apparent that the current definition of Harris Tweed was problematic.

In 1930 James Macdonald, who had previously worked as a Harris Tweed producer out of the back of a warehouse on the corner of Francis Street and Kenneth Street, set up a mill on Cannery Road, in the one-time canning factory. At first, James Macdonald had depended on the use of millspun yarn from the mainland, importing large amounts of it. But he changed his stance and campaigned to exclude millspun yarn from the trademark definition. He broke new ground by establishing the first 'vertical' mill – one where all the processes: carding, spinning and finishing are handled in one place – on the island in 1933. He later moved to Oban where he, bizarrely, challenged the very tweed definition he had successfully helped fight for.

In the late 1920s, other independent producers were also

The Queen meets Kenneth Mackenzie in 1956

becoming more prominent in Stornoway and they too would play a part in changing the trade mark. Colin Orrock set up Maclennan and Maclennan. Smiths of Peterhead also set up at the same time. They had been guilty of sending millspun yarn across the water and then receiving greasy tweeds back on the mainland for finishing. Another independent producer was David Tolmie, who would become chairman of the Lewis Harris Tweed Association. As such, he brought together all those who were against excluding imported millspun yarn from definitive Harris Tweed. This Association was soon leading the way in a dispute with the HTA over the definition.

As the industry evolved, local mills became dominant and the number of individuals involved contracted. There was tension amid long-running allegations that crofter-producers awaiting their yarn were kept hanging on for a long time by the mills.

In 1934, the amended definition came into effect, allowing yarn spun in mills on the island to be labelled as Harris Tweed. It restricted all the processes to the isles and also stipulated that tweeds must be woven at the crofter's home. Looms were removed from Stornoway mills and any other groupings of looms throughout the island were broken up.

Kenneth MacKenzie Ltd and SA Newall and Son both joined the move to 'vertical' mills. Stornoway also saw the establishment of a new mill: Messrs Thomas Smith and Co.

The 1942 Concentration of Industry Orders saw Thomas Smith's dyeing and finishing business shut down for a time, with the work transferring to Kemp and Co. Large sections of the spinning operations at both Newalls and MacKenzies were closed.. In 1946 James Macdonald left his company and went to Oban. Weaving colonies had appeared in Stornoway – groups of sheds on Cannery Road, Westview Terrace, and Inaclete Road – as a way to get round the problem of weaving not being allowed in council houses. They were built on Stornoway Trust land and had to be half a mile or less from the weaver's home, thereby acting as a stand-in for the shed on the weaver's croft.

The Clansman Tweed Company was set up by Dr David Tolmie – a nephew of the HTA chairman – around 1950. They were prominent users of mainland-spun yarn, as were Maclennan and Maclennan, although Clansman did try to

Bales of wool on Number 1 Pier with the art deco Maritime Buildings, now demolished, in the background

go over to Orb tweeds towards the end of the decade.

With a decline in the market came job losses. But confidence grew again in the 1960s and all three companies expanded. The Harris Tweed market was booming by 1965. Changes to the weavers' colonies were also under way then, with new colonies established in the light of official criticism over their location. Funded by the Harris Tweed Association and free to weavers, sheds were established "within reasonable distance" of the weavers' homes. They were set up on Rigs Road, Tolmie Terrace and Westview Terrace. The Cannery Road colony was improved.

Production fell 10 per cent in 1967, reducing the mills to week-on week-off working. Then in 1969, Kenneth Mackenzie Ltd – at that time big exporters of Harris Tweed

- were taken over by the Scottish English and European Textiles Group. Most of the small independent producers went out of business while the larger concerns survived by merging and making changes.

Amalgamations began in 1970 amid a dramatic decline in the industry. In 1974, James Macdonald's closed. Kenneth Mackenzie Holdings made an offer for their interests. HIDB commissioned research on a new double-width loom and proposals for reshaping the industry were gathering pace from 1975. Clansman, who had been spread over a number of sites on Rigs Road and Bells Road and badly needed rationalising to become more efficient, went into receivership in 1989. Kenneth Mackenzie also saw more redundancies. More amalgamations, closures and sales followed.

Pictured left, Cromwell Street around 1950 – Starting on the left hand side of the photograph is the east side of Cromwell Street:-

Numbers 29-31: The shop that is only partly in view is that of John Macdonald, general merchant; with a close entrance next to it. Both the close and the shop are now subsumed into the chemist's shop of KJ Macdonald later run by his daughter, Mrs Isobel Conning.

Numbers 25-27: one doorway then led to upstairs domestic accommodation and is now the main entrance to drapers Murdo MacLean & Sons Ltd currently run by his great grandson John Maclean

Number 23: then James Mackenzie & Sons which became Woolworths in 1999 and in 2009 M & Co.

Number 21: F W Woolworth from 1938 until 1999 when it became Furniture World.

Number 19: then the Furniture Department of Murdo Maclean & Sons Ltd, later Nazir Bros furnishings store, and since 1999 the Stornoway Library.

Numbers 11-13: At the time of the photograph this was the Club Bar, formerly Hugh Matheson's Lewis Provision Store and subsequently MacCallum's Bar, the Neptune Bar, Cromwell's bar, O'Neill's and now MacNeill's.

In the distance at the neck of the Narrows can be seen the corner and shop of George Stewart (the round window on the 3rd floor still exists), now Sports World and next to that what was then the butcher's shop of Iver MacAskill (number 7,) now The Western Isles Credit Union. Next, the Lido Cafe, then owned by the Cabrelli brothers, Andrea, Domenico and Luigi and later his daughter, Mrs L M Scaramuccia (number 5), later the Health Food Shop and now Here's Health; next to that can be seen the roof and gable end of Waverley Buildings, with the Waverley Hotel above and at ground level the radio and cycle shop of K D Bain, now the Stag Tea Room, and Burton's Corner with the Burton Tailors shop, now D M Campbell, bookmaker.

In the centre right of the picture stands the building often still called The Town House which stands on the site of the former Tollbooth or town hall. At the time of the photograph the shop in these premises named Donald Macaulay, Draper and Outfitter was owned by his son Norman and the house above by Gerrardo Capaldi who had the Central Cafe at 12 Cromwell Street in the Narrows. From 1958 the shop was occupied by the electrical shop Maciver & Dart and subsequently the Town House Café, now the Golden Ocean Restaurant.

On the right of the picture are the original railings to Perceval Square. removed in 1971 to allow for the widening of the Cromwell Street-North Beach junction and to open up the square.

A few years later – A view down Cromwell Street in June 1959
© The Scotsman Publications Ltd. Licensor www.scran.co.uk

This aerial view of Goathill was taken on June 30, 1930. In the centre of the picture is the Lewis Hospital, and the Lewis Poorhouse, with the former slaughterhouse just down the road from the Poorhouse.

This aerial view of Stornoway was taken on August 12, 1945, from 1800ft. The steamer Lochness is at No 1 Pier with m.v. Lothdale at No. 2 Pier. South Beach Quay is occupied by military buildings as is the Castle Green. The hangars in the distance were sent to Iraq in 1955

Piping down the years

The Lewis Pipe Band was formed on July 5, 1904. It first wore Hunting Stewart Tartan (Royal Stewart from 1926) and Matheson Badges presented by Major Duncan Matheson. The tunics were Bottle Green. Each band member paid 6d (2¹/₂p) per week to band funds over the years. From the beginning the Band's constitution stated that no charge would be made for their services and this is still the case, although donations are welcomed.

By the mid 1960s the Band was in a fragile state with few playing members and the uniforms and equipment were past their best. Under the auspices of the local Rotary Club a determined attempt was made to revive the group. A scheme was devised where every employee in Stornoway was asked to contribute 6d per week from their wages. Almost everyone agreed to this and within six months there were sufficient funds to purchase 21 uniforms; four sets of pipes; three side drums, two tenor drums and one bass drum at a total cost of £1,740. The reformed Band first paraded on Saturday 25 June 1966.

In addition to the weekly collection, the Band received donations from individuals and local businesses. One generous benefactor was Bain, Morrison & Co, timber merchants. Family member John Morrison, of Assynt House, was a founder member and later Treasurer of the old Band. To mark his life-long association with the Band, the committee chose Ancient Morrison as their new tartan. The Morrison Crest was chosen for the Band's Cap Badge and Plaid Brooch.

The Drum Major's Sash was presented to the Band in 1935 by Pipe Major John M. MacDonald of the Rhodesian Regiment. He was a member of the MacDonald family of Stoneyfield Farm, near Stornoway, and later became the Mayor of Bulawayo. The Sash carries the Crests of Bulawayo, the Burgh of Stornoway, the Seaforths and the 2nd Rhodesian Regiment. In 1993 the cost of restoring this historic item was met by the Stornoway Round Table.

The present Drum Major's Mace was presented to the Band in 1993 by the local branch of The Royal British

South Beach 1953... in the background the Old Caley Hotel, as Lewis Pipe Band march past

Legion. It replaced the original Mace which dated from 1926 when the Band's first Drum Major, Alex Murray, was appointed.

The Pipe Major's Pipes were gifted to the Band in the late 1960s. In 1998, a donation from the family of the late P. M. Angus (Boxer) MacLeod was used to refurbish the Pipes and add Silver Tuning Slides. The Pipe Major's Banner was presented by Bain, Morrison & Co. in 1970. It is of blue silk, backed with Band Tartan, and carries the embroidered Band Crest and the initials J. M.

The Pipe and Drum Majors and Sergeants carry Highland Dirks. The Pipe and Drum Majors Dirks are more ornate. They were purchased by donations from the families of two well-known Stornowegians, Johnny 'Lux' MacLean, Band Secretary for 36 years, and John 'The Chemist' MacDonald, a long serving committee member.

In 1926, the then Committee of the Lewis Pipe band purchased a corrugated-iron building on Bells Road, Stornoway, for £150 from the Lewis Ex-Servicemen's Club, which was in liquidation, and it became the Pipe Band Hall. It was a popular venue for a number of organisations,

including the Boy Scouts and Girl Guides and was used by them for their Annual Socials. In the Second World War, the Hall was requisitioned by the Armed Forces who failed to keep the building in a reasonable condition. Even the Hall piano was badly damaged. Only a small sum of compensation was received. The Hall slowly deteriorated until, in the 1960s, it was dismantled, leaving the site on Bells Road to become overgrown

The Stornoway Trust agreed to transfer ownership of the site to the band but it used other venues in town for practices for many years. In 1993 the Band leased the site to the Lewis Citizens' Advice Bureau who placed a large temporary office unit on the site. In 2002 when the CAB moved to Westview Terrace, their former Portacabin was offered free, complete with furnishings, to the Band and this was accepted with the Committee agreeing to make a donation of £500 to the CAB for their generosity. Some of the rent money accumulated over the previous years was then used to refurbish the unit. which now provides suitable accommodation for practice sessions, to teach Piping and Drumming and also serves as a starting point for parades.

Manor Farm … agricultural centre on the site of the present Cabarfeidh Hotel

James Street in 1937 with an early Lewis Carnival parade

Above, the County Hospital and the Lewis War Memorial in the treeless interwar years.
Right, an early 20th century view of Francis Street at the crossroads with Cromwell Street.

Workmen battle to clear snow from Goathill Road near what is now the junction with Jamieson Drive on January 21 1955. The aim was to clear a route to Goathill Farm for milk supplies to the town. Elsewhere in the Highlands and Islands 'Operation Snowdrop' was the name given to the military operation to deliver food and medical supplies to snowbound districts . RAF planes flew sorties out of the Kinloss air base primarily to drop animal fodder, and the Royal Navy flew helicopters from Wick to carry supplies to villages and farms cut off by drifts more than 10 metres high. The services flew nearly 300 sorties in all to provide relief to communities in Shetland, Orkney, Caithness, Sutherland, Ross and Cromarty, and Inverness-shire. The winter of 1955 was the worst between the two Big Freezes of 1947 and 1963. Severe weather lasted from January 4-22, and returned from February 8 until March 11. Many Highland roads remained impassable until well into March. Snow was measured at 90cm deep at Drummuir Castle, southeast of Elgin. The wintry weather extended to England and Wales for long periods too, especially during the second half of February.

A miscellany of Stornoway III

■ The Masonic Lodge in Stornoway is the oldest surviving institution in the town, with a charter dating from November 10, 1767. It was officially launched on August 16, 1769 and its records extend back to that time. For most of its first 100 years it clearly formed the major institution bringing together all those involved in the rapid development of Stornoway, filling a vacuum left by the lack of other local institutions. For its first 60 years or so, the Masters tended to be paid officials, such as Comptrollers or Collectors of Customs, the Postmaster or the Lewis estate Chamberlain. From 1830, the private sector began to predominate with merchants, farmers, and particularly shipowners, taking the lead role.

■ Prior to the building of the present Masonic Lodge in Kenneth Street, the Stornoway Lodge Fortrose met in a building on Cromwell Street. (This was clearly called Cromwell Street in October 1822 when the building was sold but had been Oliver Street at the time of a charter on the building in 1766). One of the conditions of the Cromwell Street feu charters was that owners had "on their own expenses to build the Pier and Quay opposite their own homes, and then the same to be common," In 1815 Lodge Fortrose built a stone quay opposite their property. Two years later a gale disturbed its foundations and it was rebuilt in mainland stone at a cost of £5. This property is believed to now be 53 Cromwell Street, between the present Sardar shop and the modern shop that was formerly Presto/Safeway supermarket and Mackays clothes store. After first being rented, this building was bought by the Lodge in 1805. It was then the only public hall in Stornoway and in great demand for dances and assemblies.

■ The Foundation Stone of Lews Castle was laid on November 30, 1847 with Masonic honours. The brethren of the Lodge Fortrose walked along Kenneth Street and Francis Street and then up the new road created to the castle site. The stone was laid with several coins, documents and books, along with the names of the Masonic office-bearers concealed in a cavity in the stone. There had been earlier

direct links with the landowner of Lewis. The Lodge derives its name from Kenneth, Sixth Earl of Seaforth and Viscount Fortrose. His brother Francis Humberston Mackenzie who inherited the Isle of Lewis in 1783 and died in 1815, was the Grand Master of the Lodge from 1797.

■ The site for Stornoway's Town Hall was chosen in 1898 – it was the yard attached to Carn House, including a coach house, stable and coal store. Carn House was demolished in the 1950s and is now the garden attached to the Town Hall!

■ The Masonic Lodge in Kenneth Street was the initial site proposed for the school which became The Nicolson Institute. Donald Munro, Chamberlain of the Lews, wrote to the lodge in January 1871 saying that he felt the existing building was below the standards of Lodges elsewhere. He suggested a new site in Cromwell Street explaining that an architect was expected on "the first steamer from the south" and commenting he was suggesting the alternative site "in the event" of the architect "fixing upon the Masonic Buildings" as "a suitable site for The Nicholson's Institution". The Lodge convened a committee, conferred with Mr Munro, locally nicknamed the Shah, and politely refused to move.

■ The plan for a Lewis Hospital took shape after a meeting in Stornoway in March 1892. The first patient was admitted in February 1896 after a successful fundraising campaign allowed the building of two wards, each with six beds, and an operation room. A laundry and mortuary were added later. Furnishing for the wards and other items of equipment were provided by Mr J Ross Robertson of Toronto. He was a grandson of Mr Hector Sinclair of Goathill Farm, who had been a leading Mason in Lodge Fortrose. J Ross Robertson was first a pioneering journalist and then a successful newspaper and book publisher in Canada, becoming one of the most prominent Canadians of his generation. He became Canada's leading Mason and devoted himself and, following the death of his only daughter in 1883, provided constant financial and personal

support to the Hospital for Sick Children in Toronto. Between 1883 and his death in 1918 he gave C$500,000 to that hospital. He visited the Lewis Hospital in 1898, saying it was "simply perfect in its arrangement and plan" from his 17 years of experience of hospitals throughout the world.

■ By 1856, the Lews Castle Gardens were well-established and nationally regarded and The Gardeners' Chronicle sent a reporter north to see the prodigous display. The Gardeners' Chronicle was founded in 1841 by several horticulturalists – Joseph Paxton, designer of the Crystal Palace in London; Charles Wentworth Dilke; John Lindley and William Bradbury. A newspaper, with both national and foreign news, it also included vast amounts of material sent in by gardeners and scientists. Prominent contributors included naturalist Charles Darwin and botanist Joseph Hooker. By 1851, the circulation of The Gardeners' Chronicle was 6500 compared to the Observer at 6230, and The Economist at 3826. The Gardeners' Chronicle reporter reported a profusion of many kinds of flowers, roses and fruit, particularly peaches, nectarines, pears, plums, cherries and grapes, in the gardens and glasshouses.

■ James Disher, a merchant from Dundee, came to Stornoway in 1873 and stayed in Stag Road. He became known as "Stornoway's own McGonagall" because of his prolific writing of verse – he became the official Bard of Lodge Fortrose – and commemorated, amongst other things, the Great Whale Hunt of June 20, 1869. He left Stornoway in 1887 and died, aged 96, in 1920.

■ Ships of a considerable size were built in Stornoway before the Matheson era which saw the construction of the Patent Slip in Newton. Few records survive but a 200 ton vessel, the Lord Macdonald, was launched in 1813. This was described at the time as the largest vessel ever built in the Hebrides. In 1818, a brig of 140 tons was built in the town – this was ordered by a shipowner registered in Cardiff, Wales, suggesting the town had a widespread reputation for shipbuilding.

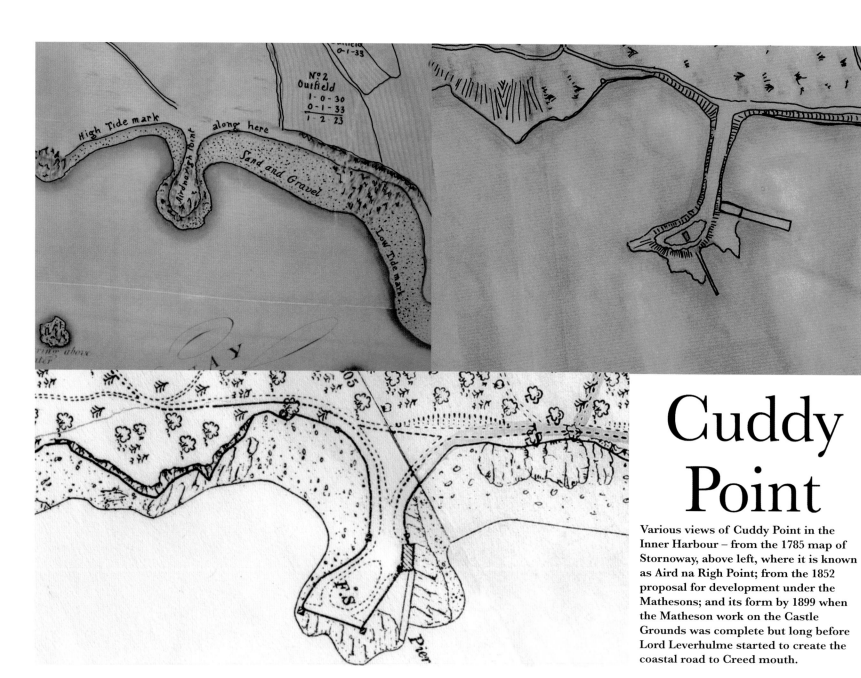

Cuddy Point

Various views of Cuddy Point in the Inner Harbour – from the 1785 map of Stornoway, above left, where it is known as Aird na Righ Point; from the 1852 proposal for development under the Mathesons; and its form by 1899 when the Matheson work on the Castle Grounds was complete but long before Lord Leverhulme started to create the coastal road to Creed mouth.

Echoes of the past have been heard again in Stornoway in recent years as work by the Stornoway Amenity Trust and the Stornoway Trust led to improvements in both the town and in the Lews Castle grounds. The Herring Girl statues, seen right on North Beach and South Beach quays were unveiled in 2003 and 2004. Sculptors Charles Engebretsen and Ginny Hutchison look on as Sandy Matheson, the Lord Lieutenant of the Isles, unveils the North Beach statue. Above is the Matheson Monument, restored and formally reopened in September 2006. Various descendants of the Matheson family of landowners were present for the first time since the sale of the Isle of Lewis to Lord Leverhulme in May 1918. The area around the monument was cleared and landscaped with additional paths being created.

With grateful thanks

The compilation of this book would not have been possible without the help of a great many people in Stornoway.

In terms of organisations, thanks must go to the Stornoway Library staff, particularly over access to the maps; and also to the staff of the Stornoway Trust and its land records; to the Stornoway Port Authority; and to Museum nan Eilean, as well as to the staffs at the National Archive and the National Library of Scotland. Great use was made of the regular publications and web-site of the Stornoway Historical Society, without whose tireless endeavours the community would be much poorer culturally, as well as of some of the publications of the Islands Book Trust.

The photographs came from many sources, but particularly the collections of John Macqueen, of Rodney Long, the Harris Tweed Authority, of Margaret Macinnes, and of the Van Der Werff family. Special thanks to Tracey Whisker for the Metagama picture on Page 89. There is, as always, the massive contribution made by the Stornoway Amenity Trust and those involved with it.

Individually, there were essential contributions from Sandy Matheson in particular, as well as from Melissa Silver for research, proofreading and general assistance; Katie Smith for compiling the tweed chapter; John MacQueen for the information on the Lewis Pipe Band; Donnie "Oscar" Macleod for documents and information relating to Lodge Fortrose; John Marsden for guidance on medieval Lewis; and Sophie Vaudoux for additional editorial advice. Any errors that remain are the responsibility of the editor.

The main picture on the back cover was taken by Fred Silver from top of the tower of Lews Castle

Bibliography and main references

Martin Martin: A Description of the Western Isles of Scotland circa 1695 Birlinn Ltd, Edinburgh 1999

John Baldwin, essay Hunting Pilot Whales: Whaling and the Hebrides The Islands Book Trust The Islands Book Trust, Isle of Lewis 2008

Mary Miers: The Western Seaboard The Rutland Press, Edinburgh 2008

John Marsden: Galloglas Tuckwell Press Ltd, East Lothian 2003

The Herring Girls in Stornoway: A lifestyle gone but not forgotten The Stornoway Amenity Trust 2004 & 2006

John Marsden: Somerled and the Emergence of Gaelic Scotland Tuckwell Press, East Lothian 2000

Finlay Macleod: Togail Tir Marking Time The Map Of The Western Isles Acair Ltd, Stornoway 1989

Christopher Burgess: Ancient Lewis and Harris: Exploring the Archaeology of the Outer Isles Comhairle nan Eilean Siar, Isle of Lewis 2008

George Broderick and Brian Stowell: Chronicle of the Kings of Mann and the Isles George Broderick, Edinburgh 1973

W. C. Mackenzie: History of the Outer Hebrides The Mercat Press, Edinburgh 1974

Peter Symes: James Alexander Stewart Mackenzie Portrait of a private note issuer International Bank Note Society Journal Volume 37, no. 1, 1998

Donald J. Withrington and Ian R. Grant: The Statistical Account of Scotland Vol. XX The Western Isles EP Publishing Limited, Wakefield 1983

Ian Armit: The Archaeology of Skye and the Western Isles Edinburgh University Press Ltd, Edinburgh 1996

Stornoway – A quick tour around the town's past The Stornoway Trust 2004

James Shaw Grant: A Shilling for Your Scowl – The history of a Scottish legal mafia Acair Ltd, Stornoway, 1992

Janet Hunter: The Islanders and the Orb – The history of the Harris Tweed Industry 1835-1995 Acair Ltd, Stornoway, 2001

Catherine Mackay: It Must Be Stornoway – The Story of the Pier and Harbour Commission 1865-2004 Argyll Publishing 2008

Victoria Silver: Stornoway's Hollywood Years; article in EVENTS newspaper, November 2005

William R. Foulger: The Lewis Combination Poorhouse; article in Islander Winter Magazine, 2005

W. C. Mackenzie: The Book of the Lews; Alexander Gardner, Paisley, 1919

David R. MacGregor: Fast Sailing Ships 1775-1875 Nautical Publishing Co. Ltd, Lymington, Hants 1973

J. Campbell-Smith: Annals of Lodge Fortrose first published 1905; republished 2008

Nick S. Robins and Donald E. Meek: The Kingdom of MacBrayne, Birlinn, Edinburgh 2008

Elizabeth Bray: The Discovery of the Hebrides Voyages to the Western Isles 1745-1883 Scotland Birlinn Ltd, Edinburgh 1996

Donald Munro: A Description of the Occidental i.e Western Isles of Scotland Birlinn Ltd, Edinburgh 1999